LIKE POPPIES DO

A Memoir of Resilience and Rebirth

CHELSEA SIMPSON

Published in Savannah, Georgia by Marigold Press Books.

Marigold Press Books titles may be purchased in bulk for educational, business, fundraising, or sales promotional use. For information, please email marigoldpressbooks@gmail.com

Fonts and stock images licensed for commercial use.

Author: Simpson, Chelsea
Title: Like Poppies Do: A Memoir of Resilience and Rebirth
ISBN: 979-8-9939178-2-5
Library of Congress Control Number: 2025927404

Cover Design: Jodi Caggige
Book Design: Russ Davis, Bravo Book Design

Printed in the United States of America

ACKNOWLEDGMENTS

This book was not written in isolation. It was written in the spaces where love met survival, where hope flickered quietly, and where people chose to stand beside me when I could not stand on my own.

To my daughters—you are the reason I am here. In moments when I honestly saw no reason to keep going, you became my reason. Your existence pulled me back toward life when everything in me wanted to disappear. You reminded me that love could still be stronger than fear, and that choosing to stay, to heal, and to keep moving forward mattered. Every word in this book carries you with it.

To my mom, my first and forever cheerleader—thank you for believing in me when I could not believe in myself. When my confidence was shaken and my voice felt small, yours never wavered. Your faith in me became a steady light I could return to again and again.

To my dad, who helped bring this dream into reality— thank you for your encouragement, your support, and your willingness to stand behind this work. Your belief helped turn an idea born from pain into something tangible and true.

To my aunt, who walked beside me with quiet strength through the final stretch—your presence, steadiness, and unwavering support carried me across the finish line. I could not have done this last part without you.

To the women in my life—friends, family, and acquaintances—who showed up in ways both seen and unseen: thank you. Through conversations, check-ins, encouragement, and grace, you helped hold me together. Each act of kindness became another small stitch in the fabric of this book.

To Rebekah, who patiently walked through this manuscript with me line by line—thank you for your time, your honesty, and your refusal to let me quit when the work felt too heavy. Your belief in this story helped me believe in it too.

To Andreas, my love and my heart—thank you for loving me in every version of myself. For supporting me when I was low, celebrating me when I was high, and standing steady through anger, joy, and everything in between. Thank you for keeping our home safe and grounded during late nights and long stretches when this work pulled me away. Your love made space for this book to exist.

And finally, to myself—to younger Chelsea—who made choices that led us into deep pain, but who also found the courage to choose something different. You were the one who decided to leave. The one who chose healing. The one who kept going when it would have been easier to stay silent. This book is proof of your resilience.

Like poppies, we do not bloom because the ground is gentle. We bloom because we are resilient. Because we push through what tries to bury us. Because even after devastation, color and life insist on returning. This book is my offering to that truth—and to everyone still finding their way toward the light.

CONTENTS

Prologue

A Model of Strength

I don't recall when I started to feel confident—this sure of myself. I adjusted my fitted black dress, checked my red lipstick in my phone's reflection, and took that first step into the convention room. It was cool compared to the balmy summer heat of Savannah, Georgia. I was one of the first people to arrive, and the clicking of my heels echoed in the large, mostly empty room. Making my way over to my company's sponsor booth, I began ensuring everything was set up according to protocol.

"Hey, Chelsea, my queen, how ya been?"

I looked up to see Bunny, one of my favorite newscasters in the city, getting set up to capture the already building energy of leadership.

I flashed her a big smile, "It's great to see you! I've been well."

And it was true—I had been well in recent years. I was a long way from the girl I once was. No longer uncomfortable in my skin, or shy, or cowardly. No, I stood tall these days.

I floated around the room as it began to fill—shaking hands with the mayor, reminding the CEO of a prominent company that we had a meeting next week, speaking with the head of a non-profit who invited me to give a speech to her company. Before any of us chatty southerners realized, it was time to start. I found my seat and settled in, eager to learn.

Surrounded by some of the wealthiest and most influential individuals I had ever encountered, I found myself immersed in the conference. The first few speakers reviewed some of the basics on leadership: "Find yourself a mentor." "Be sure to uplift your employees with team building." I was taking it all in stride until the keynote speaker launched in with her opening question:

"Who here has heard of the benefits cliff?"

She was a well-dressed African-American woman, her black hair smooth and shiny; it seemed to glide with her as she spoke, not one strand out of place. She had an air of complete comfort and confidence. She reminded me of my newfound sense of self.

With a proud stance, she changed to her next slide that listed a series of definitions. "The 'benefits cliff' refers to a situation where a small increase in a household's income results in a significant loss of government benefits, such as food assistance, housing subsidies, healthcare coverage, or childcare assistance. This can create a financial disincentive for low-income individuals and families to earn more money, as the increase in income does not compensate for the loss of benefits, leaving them financially worse off than before."

She began recounting the struggles of a single mother with two children balancing the risk of losing government aid against the possibility of a raise.

I scoffed out loud at the statement, so loud that my coworker next to me asked,

"Are you okay?"

"Oh… yes." I faked a smile and turned back to the presenter feeling suddenly like my dress was a bit too tight to breathe.

I couldn't help but steal a glance around the room. Did these affluent individuals truly understand the weight of such a decision? Did they comprehend the real-life implications of these calculations?

I sat there, glued to my chair, feet firmly planted to the ground beneath me as if this could somehow stake my claim for the right to be there. Forcing a pleasant demeanor on my face, my mind was swept up in a whirlwind of confusion and generations of pain. I was no longer in the present day, my mind propelled itself to another place, another time, but a familiar story of a bird rising from the ashes to fly again. The lyrics of a Taylor Swift song echoed in my head: *I'm getting tired even for a phoenix.* It was as if I was teetering on the edge of my current reality and my daunting past, my heart racing and the ground ready to open up and swallow me. All it would take to send me plunging right back down to darkness would be a good gust of wind.

It hit me—she was telling my story.

I knew this "hypothetical" struggle all too well. Just last week, I had found myself in the same position—a single mother of two, grappling with the harsh realities of poverty. Do I ask my boss for that raise so I can change my future—our future? The price to pay was hefty: no longer being able to afford quality childcare. How could I ever advance if I didn't have a reliable place for my children to go while I put in the hard work to achieve such things? The speaker's words resonated deeply within, stirring up memories of my own difficult choices and sacrifices.

While I knew the story she told, while I lived the story she told, I found myself still learning. Slide after slide increased my feeling of exposure until one hit me so hard I thought *surely they all know I don't belong among "them."*

"Now I will show you how generational curses, trauma, and financial situations are the first hurdles for this example of a woman to overcome before she can even SEE a future without struggle. Let's look at the statistics…"

My cool demeanor shifted into high-gear anxiety. I had never considered my family's lineage as *hurdles to overcome* to even be in that room. I'm not really sure why I had never framed it that way. It wasn't like I thought I grew up with a silver spoon, but I guess I always thought it was just something that happened, not something that happened *to me*.

My mind flashed back to my childhood in that humble three-bedroom trailer on a dead end road off a dead end road.

I was a painfully shy little girl. I looked like some dainty version of a porcelain doll—hair such a light shade of blonde it glowed in the sun, my cheeks light pink, and my lips dark red. I wore only dresses, refusing any concept of pants until I was sixteen. The 90s trends supplied me with crazy patterns and colors—lace, large bows, or flowers adorning those lovely creations.

I cannot recall what I wore on this one particular day when I was four or five years old, but I do remember how I felt. I had mustered the courage to speak up, to confront the darkness and heavy secrets lurking in our home. With a trembling whisper of a voice, I told my mother about the pain inflicted upon my siblings and me by her current husband.

My breaking point was when he laid a hand on my baby brother. I refused to let him hurt an innocent soul any longer. So I dug deep within to shut out my fear and spoke up.

My mother, our hero, wasted no time springing into action. With a fierce determination in her eyes, she packed our bags, ready to escape the clutches of abuse. Her husband, blinded by rage and control, tried to stop her, slamming her against the hallway wall in a desperate bid to maintain his grip. Amidst the chaos and the deafening screams, my mother broke free. She gathered us—my older brother with special needs, and my little brother, who was still in diapers, and me—and started anew.

This wasn't easy, but looking back I know it was the right thing. We found ourselves in the trailer, nestled in a small military town in Hinesville, Georgia. For the next eleven years this is where I grew up. The trailer had no stove or oven; we used electric skillets to cook. There were no floors—just bare particle boards with holes in various places from a home improvement project Mom couldn't afford to finish. No central heating and air, questionable plumbing, and a problem with roaches. For my mother, that trailer represented more than just shelter; it was a sanctuary, a refuge from the storm raging outside. Though modest in appearance, the real reason she chose this home was that the neighborhood surrounding us was a haven for children to grow and thrive.

Almost all the other houses on the road were occupied by the same family. Aunts, uncles, cousins, grandparents, great grandparents—all one, big loving unit known as the Wests. Next door to us lived two little girls, one a year older than me and the other close to my baby brother's age. Their home was like a second home to me, Mrs. Pam, a second mom, and the girls, my sisters. In fact, the entire West family accepted us with open arms. My brothers befriended some of the boys in the family. We spent holidays, birthdays, weekends, and even went to church with them. I honestly owe so many of my happy childhood memories to that neighborhood, to that family.

Here we were shielded from the harsh realities of the world by a community bound together by love. We made it work. I remember many times I would dream of not having to go to the food banks or other places to live, pretending my friends' homes were my own—as if they were mansions, when in reality most were double wide trailers or single family modest homes. I didn't know that when compared to the unsafe, scary, and harmful places my mother grew up, this humble shack was a beautiful home.

My mind fast-forwarded to my own journey, one marked by trauma, abuse, and financial strain, and yet also shaped and healed by the love of family, friends, and community. I had endured a decade-long marriage to an abusive man and yet somehow escaped; I had birthed two children and managed to build a life for us, find a career, and own a home. I had spent years in therapy facing my demons, like a soldier exiting a war zone, scraping the ground inch by inch toward safety, toward home. I was more determined than ever to teach and empower my kids to live beyond the curses of past generations.

As I reflected on all I had overcome, my pulse began to slow, and I took a deep, cleansing breath. I began to see my resilience in a new light. My children were not suffering, and while we struggled in my youth, I did not suffer. My mother once confided that she was selfish before having us kids. I knew her as a model of strength, a superwoman who seemed to do it all. And make no mistake, she did—but, oh, the family curses she had to break.

I have also felt selfish at some points in my own journey. I often look to my mother as an example of how to live life with grace. Life is full of struggle, but it is all about how we handle it. My mother chose to handle it by taking the parts of her childhood that haunted her the most and ensuring we never faced them. I stared down my shadows, stripped them of their power, and rose from their ashes blazing with new strength.

The woman finished her talk, and the audience exploded into applause. I overheard people in the row behind me talking about how they never thought of that perspective of life before. The announcer released us for a 20-minute break. I stood from my seat, my mind still a bit of a haze, but I straightened my spine.

I didn't have to question if I belonged in that room—I knew I did.

As the others went to grab refreshments or find the ladies room, I sought out the speaker in the crowd. I walked straight up to her and extended my hand to shake hers. I said,

"Hello, my name is Chelsea Simpson, and you just shared my story."

The tears threatened to reach both of our eyes as she said, "It was my story too."

Chapter One

WILDFLOWERS AND OLD SOULS

My family's lineage came to light in bits and pieces, like some twisted puzzle I had to assemble from fragments of our history. As I uncovered treasured pieces of my family's past—through conversations with my aunt and uncle, my mom, family friends, long-lost secret letters, and distant memories—a bigger picture began to emerge. It was a picture painted with the hues of poverty, hardship, and resilience.

My father's family carried a quiet strength of their own. Though I wasn't raised in their household and only experienced them in glimpses, their influence still left an impression. They believed in hard work, in earning your place, in showing the world you could stand tall on your own two feet. Their discipline was rooted in faith, yet beneath their sternness lived music, laughter, and the joys of scouting. From them, I learned that strength could come not only from surviving trials, but also from building something meaningful and savoring life's simpler pleasures.

My mother's side carried a different kind of inheritance, one marked by scars of survival and sacrifice. They taught me resilience born of necessity, the courage to endure, and the determination to keep going even when the path was unkind. From my mother, especially, I learned what it meant to fight quietly, to hold a household together on sheer willpower, and to model perseverance even when love and life had not been easy.

The women I came from were slaves to either the man, the dollar, or both. They endured the harshest of realities, giving birth to stillborn babies on the edges of fields, only to return to work moments later. They took part in illegal moonshine operations during Prohibition, sold their bodies just to survive, and fled from their demons, sometimes dooming their children in the process. My mother once told me her own mother was a wandering soul, never staying in one place long enough for her to make friends in school. Determined to break that cycle, she made it her mission to give us what she never had: a stable home, lasting friendships, and memories that weren't shrouded in personal hardship.

As I dug deeper into the shadows of Mom's childhood, I uncovered things that were hard to comprehend. Like me, she grew up in cramped southern shacks, but more crowded than ours—overflowing with family, friends, or her mother's latest boyfriend. The people around her were not always the kind you could trust; their presence often brought danger and discomfort. Mom and her siblings

WILDFLOWERS AND OLD SOULS | 11

found themselves in situations no child should face, with unsettling stares and unwanted attention from men who should have known better. The weight of it all was a burden she carried alone for the entirety of her life.

* * *

FOR US, GROWING UP EVERY DAY WAS A BATTLE AGAINST THE odds. We were lower class, scraping by on whatever life threw our way. My mom worked tirelessly to make ends meet. To say we struggled would be an understatement; it was a testament to her tenacity that we survived each day.

She was the type of mother who poured her love into her children. Her life's mission was to ensure us children were raised in a loving, safe environment. She did everything she could, but sadly, generational curses did prevail at times.

My older brother had a complex diagnosis: schizophrenia and autism. He took up much of my mother's time. From doctor appointments, to emotional outbursts, to dark thoughts lurking in his mind from voices only he could hear, Mom shouldered the immense burden of being both provider and protector without complaint. With the constant pulls of three children and the special needs of my brother, she found it difficult to keep steady work. She would work odd end jobs keeping her focus on being a loving, present mother to us children. Many months we survived off government aid, the charity of local food banks or churches, and the child support only my father sent, as my brothers' fathers were either not in the picture or unreliable.

I recall coming home one day from school and finding Mom gathering all the knives in the kitchen. I sat down my bookbag and asked,

"Hey, Mom, whatcha doing?"

Mom glanced up at me, her eyes heavy with exhaustion and worry, yet she still managed to say,

"Hey, Baby Girl, how was school?"

I caught her up on the latest silly sixth-grade drama and the exciting new poetry assignment in English class. She listened and packed, the clinging of the knives and other random objects chiming from time to time.

"Baby Girl, will you grab one of these boxes and follow me?"

I lifted a box, and we walked across the overgrown grass in the backyard, the weeds making the exposed skin on my legs itch. I wondered what we were doing, but I waited to ask. She opened the trunk of a broken down, rusty, old red car we had discarded like a bad memory and instructed me to put the box in as she put in hers. She closed the trunk, leaned against the car, and, pushing back her tears, explained:

"Your brother's disability has escalated. I had to pick him up early today because he shared with a teacher at school that the voices in his head have been telling him to do bad things."

The pupils of my eyes dilated, and the hair on my arms stood up.

"Baby… they told him to hurt us, so we have to keep all the dangerous objects locked away for a while—just until we can get his medicine regulated. I need your help keeping an eye on him. Can you help Mommy do that? I know you are the younger sister, but you are just so aware. Can you help me watch your brother?"

This was the first time I could remember my mom asking me to look out for my brother. It was an unspoken promise, one I still keep to this day.

*   *   *

MIDDLE SCHOOL MARKED A TRANSITIONING TIME IN MY LIFE and for our family unit as a whole. As I began to grow, it felt like I was leaving behind the image of the porcelain doll I had always known. My skin started changing, and I noticed small blemishes that seemed to appear out of nowhere. My face, once round and innocent, began to lose its childhood softness, and I could see the sharper angles forming in the mirror.

The most alarming changes came in my body. My hips widened, encouraging creepy remarks from older men: "She has baby-making hips." My waist curved and became soft and squishy. Most noticeable, however, was my chest. In the span of the summer between 7th and 8th grade I filled out more than any of us could have anticipated, often being mistaken as much older. I was suddenly aware of how different I looked compared to the other girls around me. While they seemed to blossom gracefully into their new shapes, I felt big and awkward, as if I didn't belong in this new body. The transformation was confusing, and it consumed my thoughts and defined my sense of self. I felt like my body was betraying me, making me stand out in ways I didn't like.

By the time I started my monthly cycle, Mom and I had a new tradition. We would watch romcoms, snuggled up on her waterbed with chocolate and popcorn in tow. The movies filled the screen and my mind with a lighthearted, idealized version of love. I was learning key lessons my single mother simply couldn't teach me—some realistic, others more fanciful. These films typically emphasized the idea that love is both magical and unpredictable, often arriving when we least expect it and in the most surprising of ways. They showed that love can be messy, filled with misunderstandings, and yet ultimately worth the journey. This concept of love was my ticket to escaping the daunting everyday tasks that would soon make me more of an adult than a child.

In 9th grade, the war on Iraq had brought new jobs for civilians in our small military town. The soldiers were running training exercises on base to prepare them for a variety of terrorist attacks. Mom was able to secure one of the best paying jobs she had in a while through these opportunities. I can still hear the excitement in her voice as she told me the news,

"Baby girl, guess what?"

My eyes lit up from her tone. "What?"

"I got a new job on base! It pays really well, and I'll be able to get those Sperry shoes you've been asking for now! It will be in the afternoons and into the night so I'll need your help with your brothers."

"Oh my goodness, Mom! That is exciting. Of course I can help!"

Mom was going to be an actress of sorts, dressing up as a terrorist during the soldiers' field exercises.

I was going to take care of Kurtis and Kerwyn all afternoon and evening.

Looking back, I see this was a big burden for a young girl to take on. But that is what we did, we helped each other. Since I was old enough to help with my brothers and the house, Mom could earn a better income to help give us a leg up.

So I did.

Because I had to prepare the majority of the meals now, I taught myself to cook. Mom did the cleaning while we were at school, and I picked up where she left off after I finished my homework in the afternoons. We took shifts like spouses, her talking Kurtis through his meltdowns and giving Kerwyn a listening ear, and me being the one they confided in at night before bed.

Days passed, and money did start to flow. I gave my room a teen face lift, received the entire Twilight collection of books, with the Edward poster, and bought some of the trending clothes on sale. And oh, how I treasured them! The hours were long, however, and I started to miss my mom.

One night I decided to do something special for her, in hopes of breaking up the monotony of lonely evenings at home with my brothers. It was a few days after Thanksgiving, and we still had leftovers from the feast. I gathered my brothers and devised a plan.

"Guys, Mom has been working so hard. We should do something special for her tonight when she gets home!"

"Like what?" Kurtis asked in a monotone voice.

"I think we should clean the house real well, make up her bed, warm up the leftover Thanksgiving, light candles and surprise her."

"We can put on a show too!" Kerwyn chirped enthusiastically.

The plan was hatched, and we were all in agreement: Tonight, Mom would be treated like a queen. We divided the tasks and got to work preparing everything. Furniture was polished, table set, wildflowers picked, pictures drawn, and performance rehearsed. All that was left was for Mom to arrive. The evening settled in, the sun set, the hours ticked by, and no sign of Mom. We kept looking out the window and with every set of headlights we saw approaching, we would warm up her plate. By the time she arrived we had warmed the food so many times the stuffing was crunchy.

Mom shuffled in from the cool night air, her favorite long, orange knitted scarf wrapped in a pile around her neck, yet not high enough where we couldn't see her eyes light up. We all yelled in unison: "SURPRISE!" Her face was all the confirmation I needed to know—we had done well.

I am not sure how she stomached it, but she even ate that crunchy stuffing.

I loved my mom and brothers so deeply. I wanted to bring smiles to their faces, but when I would lay my head down at night I would wonder, who brought a smile to my face? The books I read, the movies I watched told me it was love—so I believed them. Meticulously planning out exactly what married life would look like, I fantasized about all the joys love would bring me. How this would be the happiest time in my life.

By the time I began to date I was 15 going on 23. I was a typical teen, thinking I knew it all, and no one could tell me differently.

When my date's mom would bring me home, I'd have her drop me off at my neighbor's house, ashamed of them knowing where I lived. It wasn't until my first serious relationship that I let down some of those shallow defenses.

Tyler Mason was a grade ahead of me but lived in a neighboring city even smaller than my own. I met him through church, and once we hit it off there was no turning back. He was that classic good ol' boy with a country accent so thick I took pride in being one of the few who could understand him when he spoke. He sported short blonde hair and eyebrows to match. Like me, puberty hit him hard, filling out his body ahead of the other boys. His cheeks were almost always rosy red, and his clear blue eyes would twinkle when he looked at me. But the thing that attracted me to him the most was his sharp mind. The boy could talk on such deep levels my head would spin.

This is a quality in men that would get me in lots of trouble over my lifetime.

Our relationship lasted about three school years. We were both the type of people who were called "old souls" by everyone we met. Together we faced the world—he too had a troubling childhood, and this made it easy for me to open up to him. We would spend hours upon hours talking about anything and everything—nature, philosophy, politics, and pop culture. He had a way with words and a protective demeanor that made me feel safe. He was my first love—a title that still holds a high honor in my book to this day.

It was a fall afternoon and, like many times before, his mama had invited me over for dinner after church. I could tell Tyler was nervous about something, and the way his kid twin brothers were picking at him I knew there was something up his sleeve. When we parked in the dirt driveway, he looked over at me and smiled.

"I have a sur'prize for ya." His eyes twinkled with every word.

I smiled. He took my hand to help me out of the car and proceeded to lead me towards the back part of his property avoiding the mucky Georgia clay.

"Close yer eyes…"

"What?!" I giggled but succumbed to his wish.

I could hear the nervous smile in his voice, "Open 'em."

Before me stood a huge, live oak tree. The massive branches reached high into the sky and draped all the way to the ground, covered in Spanish moss, becoming an enclosed fairytale land. On the ground was a blanket spread out with a basket, candles all over, and glassware.

My heart began to race as he led me over to the blanket. We stayed there, sharing food and conversation until the stars lit up the sky and the crickets sang. Conversation led to kissing, and kissing led to making out, and making out led to his little brother busting us.

This was it, this was what I saw in the movies. We had reached *love,* and my heart was so full it could explode.

What the movies don't show you is what happens next.

After that magical night, our relationship seemed to erupt into something unstoppable. We'd tasted intimacy, felt the pull of love, and suddenly, it was as if nothing else mattered. Our teenage bodies, driven by desire, took over, and every stolen moment together became an intoxicating whirlwind of exploration and new sensations. The heat between us grew wild, like a forest fire that couldn't be contained. The desire burned so fiercely that we made a decision, a choice that felt as natural as breathing, we would be each other's firsts.

In my mind, I had painted the perfect picture of how that moment would be.

Cue the enchanting sound of a harp... It would be a cool spring night in Georgia, the air crisp and fragrant. The stars would shimmer like diamonds scattered across the sky, brighter than I'd ever seen before. I would be dressed in a flowing gown, delicate and beautiful, like a princess from a fairytale. He would be my valiant prince, strong and handsome. The world around us would mirror the magic of the moment—a perfect bed under the stars, surrounded by beauty and love. And in that moment, I would feel closer to him than I ever thought possible, as if the universe had aligned just for us.

The reality, though, was my first harsh lesson in "real love."

It was a quiet weeknight, if I remember correctly. The low hum of background music from HBO filled my room when my purple razor phone buzzed—naturally, it was after 6 p.m. for the free minutes.

"Hello, beautiful. What y'up to?" Tyler's familiar drawl came through.

"Just chilling after school," I replied casually.

"I've got something important to ask you," he said, his tone soft but serious.

"Okay...?" My heart quickened.

"Prom is coming up, and since I'm a junior, I can go. I found out today that you're allowed to come with me. So... would you be my prom date?"

Tears of happiness welled up as I blurted out, "YES!"

From that moment, we dove into planning every tiny detail—our colors, who would drive, the flowers, and eventually the weighty decision that prom night would be the night we lost our virginity.

In my mind, it would be nothing short of perfect, just like the dreamy image I played on repeat.

Prom night finally arrived, and while the build-up was electric, thrilling, nerve-wracking, the night took a sharp turn I didn't expect. At the dance, Tyler and I got into a huge fight. I was raised a good Christian girl, so when compared to the girls grinding on their dates, my modest dance moves must have looked like something out of a convent. Tyler was embarrassed, and he didn't hide it. He insisted I act more provocative, pressuring me to be someone I wasn't. That was the first time I truly felt the sting of a man wanting me to be anything other than who I was—other than the person he claimed to love.

I ran to the girls' bathroom, tears pouring down my face, feeling small and out of place. One of the other girls eventually coaxed me out, saying Tyler was sorry and that he wanted to make things right. He apologized, saying all the right words, and we left prom early. But I couldn't shake the humiliation, the shame swirling in my mind.

The whole drive to the secluded spot he'd picked out for our big moment, I chastised myself, wondering why I wasn't like other girls, why I wasn't enough.

Sometimes I ask myself why I still went through with it. Don't get me wrong—I don't regret Tyler being my first. He was kind, a good person, and part of me still holds a place of love for him. But I wonder why I let my mental well-being slip away, why I allowed myself to give away something so precious while I was beating myself up inside.

So there I was, on prom night, in the passenger seat of his truck, parked on a back road by the lake, beneath the stars—losing my innocence. Despite everything, the night did hold some kind of magic. We made our way back to his house afterward, sharing snacks, talking, and eventually falling asleep snuggled up on the couch. He got me home by curfew—1:00 a.m. sharp. But that night marked a shift in me, one I'd feel for a long time to come.

As time passed, the weight of life started to creep in, and the space between us grew wider. His once charming intensity turned into something darker. His political and social views became more extreme, rigid. The more he fell in love with me, the more his controlling side surfaced, gripping tighter with every passing day. He became consumed with paranoia and fearful that I might look at other guys or, worse, stop wanting him altogether.

I was already carrying the weight of so much in my life—expectations, responsibilities, struggles—and I couldn't bear the suffocating pressure of his control on top of it. It felt like I was drowning in the very thing that was supposed to lift me up. I craved freedom, the chance to breathe and live on my own terms.

It was the day after my 16th birthday when it all came crashing down. I wanted more, I wanted to experience life, to spread my wings and live fully, to become the strong woman I knew I could be. But it was painfully clear that the two—my freedom and his love—couldn't coexist. So, on a sunny, mild February day, I made a hard decision. I ended it.

Little did I know that by October, everything I thought I knew about my life—the path I was on, the person I was becoming—was about to shift in ways I could never have imagined. The entire trajectory of my world was on the verge of changing forever.

Chapter Two

HANDCUFFS AND CHERRIES

Love. Oh you allusive thing. I thought I knew you when I was only a young girl. Do you remember?

You came upon me like flushed cheeks in the crisp winter air. Causing smiles matched by giggles till my face cramped.

What did having you mean? I chased you desperately trying to define. Marking trees with symbols as if that would allow you to grow. Yet I was only left with a withering sense of self. My flourishing and blossoming ceasing till I said goodbye.

There were times I was alone, Love, going through life discovering. But I thought I couldn't live without you. I cut this time of discovery short, like a candle blown out on a 16th birthday wish. I went desperately searching again, now as a young lady.

We met, and it was hot. An all consuming flame over my entire being. This was when I knew who I was, right? No fear of the unknown to bother my steadfast sight set on you.

Not one part of me wasn't touched by you, Love. My mind was taken over by all you were. I found your fast pace and extreme highs and lows intoxicating. I let go of all I was and fell into love.

Embracing every burning ember, breathing in the warmth of your embrace. I thought you were a flame I had to keep alive, not realizing the gravity of what you were doing to me.

Being a teen girl was a fact of life I resented until I was no longer one. It wasn't long after my relationship with Tyler that I was launched into a life closer to that of a 25 year old than a teen.

I was shifting and growing bored with the typical teenage stuff, and yet I craved to be as confident as the "popular girls" at school. I wanted to glow when I laughed and walk with my head high. 16 years old, my hair was long, blonde, and messy. Not messy like a rats nest but more like how your hair falls after the perfect beach day. My body was curvy and like that of a grown woman in comparison to my petite classmates. I just simply didn't fit in with the kids my age because of both my appearance and personality. At the time I thought being popular and fitting in meant I needed to be skinny. (What the fuck did that mean? I didn't know, it was just a body type.) The state of mind I yearned for was not attached to my body size. But I didn't know that at 16. So instead I found myself drawn to older people in an attempt to find belonging.

There I was, no longer a girl but also not quite a woman. My best friend, Tina, was in town visiting her mom. Right before our first year of high school, her father moved her away, and we were both devastated. When she was in town, it was a huge deal.

We sat on her bedroom floor discussing our plans for the night...

"So what should we do?" Tina asked casually as she painted her nails navy blue, talking over KISS FM radio playing "Womanizer" by Britney Spears.

"Let's do something fun, crazy, live a little!"

The look that settled over her face was that of confusion, curiosity, and hesitation.

"I don't know, Chelsea."

"Come on, we always follow the rules! Let's be teenagers for once. We can get all dressed up and hit the town. Try to find some boys to buy us drinks!"

Tina was right to be concerned—I was in a desperate state of mind, craving not only attention but validation. I was craving it from men, not even boys because to me I was no *girl*.

I convinced her to play along. After her mom left for the local bar, as she did every night about the same time, we piled into my old beater of a car and headed out.

We went to Walmart and walked around, then drove around the city until Tina was so painfully bored she asked if we could stop by a gas station to get a fountain drink and then go home.

As we pulled into the gas station, I immediately noticed a tricked out, low rise red truck and out hopped a guy we would come to know as Cody T. This led to numbers exchanged, plans made to come over to "our place to chill." The price was for him to bring wine coolers, which we knew wouldn't be a problem—he looked about 22.

"Oh shit!" We giggled as we got in the car and rushed home to get the house ready for the guys arrival.

Once back at Tina's house, we got to work removing every picture, childhood drawing, any piece of evidence that we were kids and not 21 year olds. We devised a plan where only one of us would drink and the other would pretend to drink to be "safe."

We could have very well been kidnapped or murdered that night. Still, my favorite memory wasn't meeting Tray, the games we played, her mom busting in on us, or drinking. NO. It was after they left, I was very drunk and got sick. Tina made me Kraft Mac n Cheese, and we sat on her bedroom floor eating it and watching an old VHS tape of Animaniacs, still texting the guys. BEST mac and cheese I have ever eaten. Best friend I have ever had.

I didn't know it at the time, but Tina had endured some hard things that year she had been gone. She had already seen the darker side of men, and this is why she was so hesitant that night. I didn't pause long enough to even learn from my friend's lived experiences. Perhaps, however, someone will learn from mine.

* * *

TRAY WAS 23, AND TO ME, HE SEEMED LIKE THE MOST exciting person in the world—6'3", his eyes the perfect shade of blue, and dark brown, slightly long, shaggy hair with frosted tips. He made me laugh so hard my stomach and cheeks would hurt. He had tattoos, one of which was a set of cherubs on his chest, an angel with the script text "guided by angels," the other a devil and script that read "tempted by the devil."

He was in a wild, party-driven phase of his life, indulging in recreational drug use, which I naively dismissed as harmless fun. I was in an escape-seeking mindset, and he seemed like just the bad boy I was looking for to show me the world. I didn't understand how people were allured by cocaine and alcohol, I got my highs from love. 16-year-old Chelsea thought she saw beyond the front of that party boy, a fun, charming, jokester of a man who captured my heart. I thought I could find stability in escape. I was his angel, and he was my perfect shot of the devil.

Just like that, we were attached at the hip. Every free moment I had I would follow him like a lost puppy. I fed on the scraps of attention he gave me. I served his every whim as if I had no thoughts of my own, his wish gladly my command, all along revealing more and more of myself that he would twist and turn into his own narrative.

In the end this left me with a distorted version of myself.

* * *

IT WAS OCTOBER 2023. I WAS DRIVING THROUGH MY beautiful city of Savannah, far from the 14 years of life behind me, front windows down, wind in my hair. My Spotify playlist was on shuffle when a Kesha song started to play... "Wake up in the morning feeling like..." Quickly, I changed the song.

I ran through my mental list of things that can trigger flashbacks: red trucks, motorcycles, Statesboro, GA, men's cargo shorts, lawnmowers, the pet name "Sweetheart," mexican food, mattress stores, holding hands in Walmart... the list goes on, and this time was no exception—an old song.

Suddenly a wave of emotion came over me. It felt like I was numb, suspended under water. All I could hear was the slowing thump... thump... thump of my own pulse, along with an eerily distant chatter.

I saw my younger self and Tina hopping into my old, large, gray town car. The side had a dent and a panel missing, the brackets that once held it on looked like stitches. My CD on repeat was a special mix made by my friends—everything from early Taylor Swift to rap and heavy metal.

From the mirror hung handcuffs and an air freshener—a pair of cherries in bright red. The jelly red would catch the sunlight and something about the mix of the two, handcuffs and cherries, made me feel daring. I felt excited and nervous that night as I drove the 35 minutes to Richmond Hill. I was on the way to another party at Tray's house, dressed to kill and ready to have an adventure.

Those handcuffs and cherries set a perfectly symbolic backdrop for these parties. Tray wouldn't only invite me to grand events he hosted but would show me off like a golden prize.

We walked into a scene with Kesha playing in the background. Drugs, alcohol, grown ass adults, and no one like me and Tina. Girls half naked, with their fully developed bodies bouncing as they tried to distract their opponents in beer pong. Weed smoke filled the air, and men in the kitchen were choking down shrooms dipped in ranch. Others passed around a mirror with cocaine to snort. I thought I wanted to be like them and still unique at the same time. So I played the role of a confident woman who refused any drugs. This was the first night I told a lie to someone I loved to cover up Tray's bad influence. This was the night I lost any sense of simply being a 16 year old. As I laid under 23-year-old Tray, pressuring me to go further than I wanted, my eyes kept creeping back to the TV playing *Mr. and Mrs. Smith* in the background.

Add that to the triggers list, the movie *Mr. and Mrs. Smith.*

Later that night I insisted to Tina that nothing happened. I can still see the disappointment in her eyes as she realized her best friend was lying to her. The parties didn't end that night, however. Neither did the lies. I was swept up in a long string of people around me getting high in rundown houses, and I often fell asleep on the couch. I remember thinking that him keeping me safe from harm was love, so I slept like a baby. More times than not I'd wake before anyone else to clean and cook breakfast—no wonder he fell in love and expected such treatment.

I was tangled in the illusion of love, clinging to the reckless, heady feeling of being wanted. He was too much older, but that only made it feel more real, more important. In my mind, it wasn't just a relationship; it was proof that I was grown, that I mattered.

But my mother was no fool.

She had loved me fiercely my whole life, fought for me, protected me, and in one terrible moment, she realized I had been lying to her.

I still remember the way her face changed when she found out. The way her voice turned sharp and her hands trembled. Not with fear, but with anger, with heartbreak. And then, the slap.

"Take off your glasses," she said, voice tight.

I hesitated, but I knew better than to disobey. Slowly, I removed them, vision blurring at the edges.

Then—*crack!*

The sting burned across my cheek, sharp and sudden.

My breath hitched, but I refused to cry. I refused to let her see me break.

"You lied to me," she said, shaking her head, pacing now. "Do you have any idea what you've done? What you're throwing away?"

I stood still, my hands gripping the hem of my shirt. "I love him."

Her laugh was bitter. "You don't even know who he is, what love is."

I swallowed hard, my face still stinging. "And you do?"

That stopped her in her tracks. Her eyes, usually so warm, so full of love, were tired. Worn down.

"I know what it isn't," she said. "It isn't sneaking around. It isn't lying to the people who love you. It isn't a grown man looking at my 16-year-old daughter like she's a woman."

"He's not like that," I argued. "He cares about me. He listens. He…"

"He's a grown-ass man, Chelsea!" she snapped, slamming her hand on the table. "What does a grown man want with a girl who is still in high school?"

Silence stretched between us.

Then, without another word, she turned and started pulling open drawers, cabinets.

"What are you doing?" I asked, my stomach twisting.

She grabbed my makeup bag, my jewelry box, and the heels I had hidden in the back of my closet. "If you want to act grown, let's see how you feel without all this."

I tried to grab my things back, but she held firm. "No more makeup. No more heels. No more *anything* that makes you think you're ready for a world that will eat you alive."

Tears burned my eyes, but I refused to let them fall.

"And you're grounded," she continued. "No phone. No leaving this house. No seeing *him*. School, work, home."

I felt my world collapse in on itself. "You can't do that."

She leveled me with a look that said I didn't understand just how much power she held. "Watch me."

For weeks, she tried to pull me back. She kept me home, kept me away, hoping that if she just held on tightly enough, I would come to my senses.

But it was too late. I had already fallen.

And somehow, she knew it.

One evening, she came into my room, her expression unreadable. "I met with him today."

My stomach dropped. "What?"

She sat on the edge of my bed, exhaling slowly. "I had to see for myself. To see if he was just another man taking what he wanted or if he actually loved you."

I braced myself for another fight, another lecture. But she just looked at me—really looked at me.

"And?" I asked, barely above a whisper.

She sighed. "And he loves you."

I blinked. "So…?"

She closed her eyes for a moment, then met mine. "So I'm stepping out of the way."

Shock rippled through me. "You're… you're not going to fight me anymore?"

Her lips pressed together, and for the first time, I saw something I hadn't noticed before—fear. Not fear of him, but fear of *losing me.*

"If I push too hard," she said softly, "I will lose you completely. And I won't do that."

I stared at her, unsure of what to say.

She reached out then, tucking a stray piece of hair behind my ear. Her voice was thick when she finally spoke again.

"I just hope you don't lose yourself."

And with that, she left me to make my own choices.

Chapter Three

WINDING ROAD

In those early years, I thought I saw Tray's true self. We were young, and I believed his wild side was just a phase. I followed him like an addict, taking in his admiration, compliments and phrases like, "You are so mature for your age," as if they were my lifeline.

He was the true addict, however. We were caught in a whirlwind of thrill seeking—shallow attempts to hide feeling anything real.

After two years I grew tired of the party life. I should have seen the signs back then, that he was poison, already caught in infidelity and hooked on the power and drugs he sold. I told him I was done, he told me he would stop using drugs. Out of his love for me, Tray claimed he put them down. Shortly after, he got into trouble with the law, which seemed to force a real change. He went through the legal system, got clean, and passed all his drug tests. He started working at his father's motorcycle shop. My hope was renewed that we could have a life together.

Then, Tray proposed. Like so many girls, I had spent hours dreaming of that moment—imagining soft candlelight, romance thick in the air, and maybe even the faint sound of a harp somewhere in the background. It would be perfect, like stepping into the pages of a fairytale. But reality? Reality left me feeling foolish and naive.

Tray had never been great at keeping secrets, or at least when it came to surprises for me. He blurted out that he was planning to propose and even took me to his aunt's jewelry shop to pick up the ring. I remember standing there as he handed it to me for the first time. I stared at it, trying to feel something. Was this ring *me*? The thought passed like a shadow, but I quickly buried it and fawned over the diamond as his aunt explained the craftsmanship and the price he would have paid if it weren't for family discounts.

Just as quickly, Tray snatched the ring from my hands, closed the case with a snap, and announced, "Alright, let's go!"

I blinked. "Wait, what? I'm not getting it now?"

The proposal didn't come that day, or the next. Instead, Tray planned a dinner with both our families at Love's Seafood, a local restaurant best known as the strip club where Forrest Gump met Jenny. Romantic, right? I convinced myself it was thoughtful, in his own way. I assumed he'd propose before the dinner so we could share the news together. Wrong again.

The night of the dinner, I dolled myself up in a dress

I had saved for something special. My heart was racing with anticipation. Tray, however, had other plans. After the meal, he took me down to the water under a canopy of twinkling lights. Our mothers stood at a distance, watching with what I could only assume was pride. He sat me in a swing, dropped to one knee, and… picked up a penny.

"Look, a lucky penny," he said with a grin. "Can we go home now? It's cold."

I felt my heart sink like a stone.

When we walked back up to the restaurant, my mother's face said everything I was too ashamed to admit —disappointment, concern, and maybe even a little pity. She had pawned her jewelry to afford dinner that night, just to celebrate what she thought would be a joyous occasion. It wasn't.

On the drive home, I was desperate. I begged Tray to take me somewhere romantic. Instead, we went home. I locked myself in the bathroom, wiped away my makeup with shaking hands and stripped away that special dress. The girl who had walked into that night with dreams of twinkling lights and romance was now staring into the mirror, wondering what on earth she was doing with her life.

When I finally came out, there he was. On one knee.

"Chelsea Elizabeth Simpson," he began, "I want to spend forever with you. As you are—no fuss, no fancy clothes or makeup, no family. Just you. Will you marry me?" He called our dog Mary into the room, the ring tied clumsily to her collar.

I said yes.

Looking back now, I can see it so clearly—it was manipulative. Everything about that proposal was a reflection of who Tray wanted me to be, not who I really was. If he truly knew me, he would have understood that I loved fashion, romantic gestures, and, most of all, family. But to Tray, I wasn't a person with my own thoughts and feelings—I was the version of me he had built in his mind.

You'd think I would have seen the cracks in our relationship as we began planning the wedding, but any doubts I had vanished the moment I found out I was pregnant only two months into the engagement. Tray was adamantly pro-life, and while I'm not saying I would have made a different choice, I never even had the chance to consider one. We moved the wedding up from October two years later to June of that year. I refused to step into that hospital unwed.

We tied the knot and soon welcomed our first child, but the rifts between us only became more pronounced. That first year of marriage was nothing short of a nightmare.

During our dating years, I had seen flashes of Tray's anger, but I brushed them off, convincing myself they were just fleeting moments. Marriage shattered that illusion. His anger escalated, and our arguments turned vicious. He began blocking me from leaving during fights, trapping me in a cycle of fear and helplessness.

I was 19, living in the first brick house I had ever called home, with a newborn in my arms. But instead of feeling joy or accomplishment, I felt like I was crumbling. Tray's words, once filled with love and praise, turned sharp and demeaning. He no longer lifted me up like the queen he once promised I was. Instead, he tore me down with constant criticisms: I wasn't good enough, I didn't clean enough, cook enough, or have sex enough to be a "good wife."

Every day, I was bombarded with the message that I was the problem. Juggling a new baby, a body I didn't recognize, and a husband who had transformed before my eyes, I was drowning. I convinced myself that this was just marriage, that no one ever said it would be easy. I believed the fault must lie with me.

Desperate for stability and affection, I bent like a willow tree to Tray's every whim. He wanted me to be a stay-at-home mom, so I cut my hours. He wanted me to dress more maturely and modestly, so I overhauled my wardrobe. With each concession, I lost another piece of myself.

I was spiraling, sinking into postpartum depression so deep I couldn't see a way out. I hated my body, convinced I was failing as a mother, and certain I was failing as a wife. The weight of it all crushed me, and I learned to compartmentalize like a seasoned actress.

At work, I played a role—bubbly, happy-go-lucky Chelsea. I threw myself into proving my worth, not just to my boss and colleagues, but to myself. I worked tirelessly, climbing the ranks to manager, earning spots on special projects, and building friendships with regulars. I became the person I wanted to be, at least for eight hours a day.

But as soon as I clocked out, reality hit me like a wave. The 15-minute drive home on that dark, winding road became the most dangerous part of my day, not because of the road itself, but because of my thoughts. I often fantasized about veering into the guardrail, imagining the silence that might follow. Maybe they'd be better off without me. Maybe the emptiness would finally stop.

The car was where my mind turned on the replay. I would start running through the fights like a cruel film: the slam of doors that sounded like thunder in our small house, the way furniture would shudder and crack when it was broken over arguments, the fist through drywall that left ragged holes and an ache that no bandage could touch. I could still hear the sharp inhale before a voice raised itself, the metallic taste of panic in my mouth, the slow, terrible quiet that came after—as if the house held its breath along with me. Those scenes looped until the edges of everything blurred. My hands tightened on the wheel and my heartbeat became a second metronome counting out the hours until I could be somewhere else.

Desperate to do something right for once, I let him convince me I wanted to "explore" in the bedroom. The thing is, I wasn't some perfect saint. I'd always been curious about my own sexuality, trying to understand it and figure out what I liked. But Tray had this way of taking those small, vulnerable parts of me and twisting them into something bigger, darker. He made it feel like the new ideas were mine, like I wanted this too. Sometimes I believed him. I'd tell myself, *Maybe this is me growing, being open, being adventurous.*

But deep down, I was confused and uncomfortable.

I didn't even know who I was trying to be. I thought a good wife should be sexy, and in my mind, sexy meant graceful, delicate, like something out of the 1950s that Tray idolized. Lace, soft allure, daintiness—that's what I thought I needed to embody. I imagined myself as a pearl necklace, timeless and classic. But Tray? Tray wanted something harder, edgier. He wanted a choker.

When he started talking about "change," I thought maybe this was my chance to feel good about myself. Maybe this would make me love my body—or at least make him happy. Isn't that what good wives do? So, I went along with it. I told myself it was fine, that it would "spice things up." But I didn't feel fine.

This was the first time he brought up "alternative pleasures." I don't even want to write what came next. Ropes. Choking. Other people. Our bedroom stopped feeling like a place of connection and became something else entirely—something dark, something suffocating. A place that should have been a sanctuary of connection and intimacy became more like a torture room.

And it wasn't just the bedroom that fell apart. Longtime friendships shattered right along with whatever pieces of myself I'd been clinging to. I went dark, fast. Suicidal thoughts weren't just whispers in the back of my mind anymore—they were loud, constant. I felt like I had nowhere to go, no way out. And of course, it was all blamed on me.

I hit a crossroads. I could end it all, or I could find a way to survive. One day, I looked at my baby girl—her tiny, innocent face —and something in me shifted. She didn't deserve to grow up without a mom. So, I made a choice. I started seeing a doctor and got on medication. It helped, I guess, but if I'm being honest, I was never the same after that.

About a year later, we couldn't afford that beautiful brick home anymore and ended up moving to a smaller shotgun house in a nearby town. This was supposed to be our fresh start. I threw myself into building a new life: I quit my job, started taking online college classes, raising chickens and bunnies, and planting gardens. For a little while, I actually believed it might work, that things might get better. But the illusion didn't last long.

One day, amidst an argument Tray snatched the car keys out of my hand so hard it made my fingers ache, then hurled them into the yard. I stood there frozen, the message clear: I wasn't going anywhere. I felt trapped. Fear gripped me in a way I hadn't felt since I was a kid, flashing back to the night I watched my mom slammed against the hallway wall. Was that going to be me next? Would he do that to me in front of our child? I couldn't shake the fear, so I packed a bag. I was ready to leave, but when Tray found out, he exploded in rage.

His voice was raised in volume, but it was his words that chilled me to my core: "If you ever take my child from me, I will kill you, chop you into a million pieces, and no one will ever find your body!" He screamed it with such venom that I believed him.

Adrenaline shoved me into motion. I ran for the car as if the only map out of that house led through the driver's seat—feet pounding the gravel, hands fumbling with the handle, breath ripping in my chest.

Before I could pull the door open, he stepped in front of it. His body was a deliberate blockade; the look in his eyes was animal and exact.

Panic tunneled my vision down to the scrape of his shoe and the hot, close sound of him breathing.

Then he struck the car. His fist hit the metal with a sound that was both immediate and forever—a hollow, violent clang that rolled through the yard and lodged in my ribs. A dent spread under his knuckles, a crooked bruise in steel that would catch the light and my attention for years to come.

I stared at it and felt something in me harden and break all at once; the dent was a small, brutal monument to that night, something I would later trace with my eyes whenever I passed the driveway.

His words and the strike lodged inside me like splinters. I turned away from the car. I walked back into the house with trembling hands, fear of the unknown, my breath shallow, and my mind loud but my voice silenced. I turned away from a world that smelled of adrenaline and the metallic aftertaste of threat, confident that this was my only choice.

That wasn't the last time he said it either. That phrase became one of his favorites, repeated often enough to cement itself in my mind like a brand. Every time, it felt like the walls closed in a little more, my fear growing with each threat. I was barely 20 years old, and I didn't know how to get out or what to do—but I knew one thing for sure. I had to keep my baby safe.

After his outbursts, Tray would come to me, pleading for forgiveness, promising to change—even falling to his knees and summoning tears on cue. While this cycle had become familiar, something I had learned to navigate like second nature, I still clung to the fragile hope that he would change; that one day, the apologies wouldn't be empty, the promises wouldn't break like glass beneath my feet.

But fear kept its grip on me, whispering that I had no way out—that this was simply the life I was meant to endure. He swore he loved me and our daughter and would stop having angry outbursts. I made my mind believe him and stayed, determined things would improve. *I can fix this, I can fix him; he is the father of my child.* I introduced coping mechanisms to manage his anger and tried to teach us how to fight more constructively. We had a few manageable years, but Tray's anger and his chilling threats never fully disappeared.

To the outside world, we seemed like the perfect couple—happy, in love, and building a life together. I worked hard to hide any cracks in that illusion, covering up the truth that simmered just beneath the surface.

In 2015, I started working part-time at the family motorcycle shop, and for the first time in a long time, I felt like I'd found something I was good at. I dove into their marketing, and the business began to thrive. We even started the process of opening a tattoo shop. It was exciting on the surface, but my real saving grace came from something else entirely.

That same year, as part of my responsibilities, I organized an all-female group dedicated to hosting monthly fundraisers for local nonprofits. The idea was the events would bring new business to the shop. These women and our shared mission became my escape, a lifeline I clung to when everything else felt like it was falling apart. Through them, I found purpose, connection, and a glimpse of what life could be like beyond my walls.

I'm still friends with many of these women today, and I don't think they even realize how much they saved my life during those years. They gave me something to hold onto when I felt like I was drowning.

In abusive patterns good things never last long, so what came next was unavoidable.

It all came crashing down one evening when Tray came

home hysterical, with bloody knuckles, saying that he "fucked up." His temper now spilling over into work, he destroyed our careers at the motorcycle shop. He hurt his father, and there was no excuse for his actions.

From that day on we did not speak to his father. We walked away from the shop. I walked away from my calling.

We started over. Again.

I went back to work, landing a job at an all-female accounting firm where I steadily climbed the ladder. Tray found work at an aircraft subcontractor shop building cabinets. For a while, it seemed like we were doing well financially. We were both bringing in good money, yet somehow, every month, we came up short on bills.

Between impulsive purchases to keep up appearances, credit cards maxed out in my name because of his bad credit, and money that seemed to just vanish, our financial stability unraveled quickly. Debt piled up, and I felt like I was treading water while Tray's spending pulled us further under.

That year, everything took a turn for the worse. Tray's anger, which had simmered since he and his father's falling out, boiled over. He sought release in drugs; and with it, came a darker, more controlling side of him. His paranoia and jealousy consumed him. He isolated me from friends, fractured my relationships with family, and forbid me from being around men entirely—even at work. I shrank myself to fit his demands, focusing only on my child and tiptoeing through every interaction, desperate to avoid setting him off.

As our finances spiraled, we couldn't even afford the shotgun house anymore. Tray made the decision—barely consulting me—that we would move into a single-wide trailer his family owned in Statesboro. He framed it as an opportunity to save money and build our dream home on the land. I tried to believe him, clinging to the hope of a fresh start.

I commuted an hour each way for work while Tray started a lawn care business. When my great grandfather's inheritance came through, we paid off $35,000 in debt and were given a new car. For a fleeting moment, I thought we'd turned a corner.

Then COVID hit. The world shut down, and I found myself working full-time from home, homeschooling, and trying to hold everything together while the weight of the pandemic bore down on us. Tray was "working," but in truth, he was sinking deeper into his addiction, hiding it from me while his behavior became more volatile.

During the pandemic, domestic violence rates skyrocketed, and my home was no exception. The walls of that trailer felt like they were closing in. Imagine living through a deadly virus yet being too terrified of the person sleeping next to you to even think about it. Fear became my constant companion, a shadow that never left, even in the daylight.

Chapter Four

The Glass Castle

Nothingness, I was comfortable in this place. It was like a warm blanket and a cup of coffee on a cold winter's day. Blank and thoughtless, not dumb, not foolish. No, this was the escape I needed from my foolish choices.

Have you experienced this bliss? Have you experienced the anguish that leads to this becoming your place of bliss?

Lack of passions, dreams, care, give a fuck, love, hate, any of the great wonders of life? They were all eluding me.

I found myself in the moments of clarity where I knew; I knew that my life was shit. Everything I was building was just a glass castle.

It was the castle I wanted, in the fairytale I imagined, so I kept playing my role. Here is the thing I can not wrap my head around; it was real for me. This life I imagined was REAL for me, tangible, made of a material so beautiful that sparkled when the light shined through. Yet so fragile and dangerously painful once shattered.

In May 2020, I found out I was pregnant with our second child. The excitement was fleeting... Just 12 weeks later, I miscarried. The loss hit me like a tidal wave, pulling me under into a world of grief and trauma. It felt like I'd been forced into a tunnel with no doors or windows, no escape—just a suffocating darkness where all I could see, hear, and feel was pain. In that tunnel, negative thoughts took root and grew wild, twisting reality until I couldn't tell where the pain ended and I began. The only way out was straight through, but at the time, I couldn't even see a way forward. I was frozen in place, trapped, paralyzed by grief.

The days blurred together. I remember staring blankly at the TV for hours, the flickering images meaning nothing, or standing under the shower for so long the water turned from steaming hot to icy cold. I wasn't even numb—I was aware of the freezing water but didn't care enough to step out. I'd find myself standing over the kitchen sink, shoveling random food into my mouth without tasting it, just going through the motions. I was utterly detached from myself.

When I realized I was spiraling, I'd decide it was time to pull myself together. I'd pick a new project or a diet or tell myself it was time to chase a dream I'd let go of.

But those were surface-level distractions, band-aids for a wound too deep to reach. No matter what I did, my thoughts always circled back to the future I thought we were building—me, Tray, our babies. I had envisioned a picture-perfect life, one we were painting together. But in the wake of my miscarriage, that picture began to fade.

I sought solace in therapy, trying to process the loss and make sense of my emotions, but Tray was slipping away. He grew distant and unpredictable, his anger surfacing more often, his behavior becoming increasingly erratic. He'd stay awake for days on end, then crash and sleep for what felt like forever. His body twitched, his energy chaotic and restless. I began to suspect he was using drugs again, but every time I asked, he denied it. I wanted to believe him. I needed to believe him.

By May 2021, I was heavily pregnant with our third child, and the cracks in our life were growing into canyons. One day, while cleaning the bathroom, I found a cigarette pack tucked away in a corner. Inside, there was a small bag of white powder. My heart sank as I confronted him. This time, Tray couldn't lie. He admitted to using drugs but claimed it was just cocaine, as if that made it any less dangerous or heartbreaking.

From that point, everything felt like it was teetering on the edge of disaster. Tray's behavior became even more erratic. His anger flared at the slightest provocation, making the air in our home feel heavy with tension.

The danger became undeniable. One night, during

what was supposed to be a rare date night, Tray fell asleep at the wheel. My heart pounded as I reached over to grab the steering wheel, screaming at him to wake up. It wasn't just the drugs anymore; it was alcohol too. I started finding empty beer bottles on the floorboards of our cars. Every discovery felt like another blow, another reason to fear for my children's safety.

I felt like I was clinging to a crumbling ledge, trying to hold everything together as it disintegrated in my hands. The man I once loved, the father of my children, was disappearing before my eyes, replaced by someone I barely recognized. And yet, I kept hoping; hoping this was just a phase, hoping he would stop, hoping that somehow, we could still salvage the life we were supposed to have.

On June 28th, Tray's rage hit a terrifying new peak. He started screaming in my face while I held our newborn daughter. His threats of violence had been escalating for months, but that night, something shifted. The furniture-breaking tantrums and the holes he punched in the walls felt tame compared to the way his bloodshot eyes bore into me.

"Please, stop yelling," I whispered, clutching the baby closer. "She's sleeping."

Tray's response sent a chill through my entire body. "I could just kill you right now."

The words hung in the air like a blade poised above me, and for a moment, I couldn't breathe.

The next day, on what should have been our ninth wedding anniversary, Tray unleashed another verbal assault as soon as I woke up. I needed space and comfort so my mom came over while he was "working" and took me and the babies to dinner; Tray didn't like this. Angry that I wasn't spending our anniversary having dinner with him, he drained our bank account while I was out to dinner, texting me cryptic messages about not knowing when—or if—he'd be back that night. I came home to an empty house and spent the night pacing, sleepless and nauseated with worry. His unstable behavior wasn't new, but suddenly, everything started clicking into place.

Desperate for answers, I reached out to his mother. She hesitated before suggesting something I'd never considered. "Do you think he might be using meth?"

The signs were there, I just hadn't wanted to see them. A quick search on Google confirmed my worst fears. Then, I found pipes and drugs hidden in our home. My hands trembled as I held the evidence, realizing how deep this ran.

With his mother and stepfather's help, we staged an intervention. Tray admitted he'd been using meth for five years but refused to get help. I knew then that I couldn't stay. I packed a bag for me and the girls: clothes, diapers, formula, and the guns registered in my name. I was terrified of what he might do if he found them in the house.

That first night at my mother-in-law's, the threats started again. Tray was furious about the missing AK-47 that I had taken because it was in my name. His anger was like a bomb ticking down, and I could see his mother and stepfather unraveling as the truth of the situation sank in. They hadn't known the years of torment I had endured, and their first instinct was to smooth things over. But I knew Tray. He wasn't coming to talk; he was coming to take.

When I heard he was on his way to their house at 2 a.m., I made the only decision I could.

I packed the car in silence, careful not to wake the girls until everything was ready. "We have to go," I whispered, shaking them gently.

Their sleepy, confused faces broke my heart, but I forced myself to be strong. "I can't tell you why or where we're going, but I promise I'll keep you safe."

The road was eerily quiet as we fled, but my mind was anything but. Every fear, every possibility, every step we might take from here—it all churned in my head. But I knew I couldn't afford to panic.

This was survival. Fight and flight, all at once.

I focused on three things:

1. Find a safe place far from Tray.
2. Get help with the girls.
3. Trust no one but those who had proven themselves.

Tray had spent years isolating me, but I refused to let him leave me without support. Despite the early hour, I knew who to call.

The first call was the most important. My hands shook as I dialed, and the phone rang once, twice, three times. I held my breath, praying she'd answer.

Courtney had long since moved away from Georgia, but never from my heart. She was a fiery redhead with a presence that could light up an entire room, and a soul that radiated warmth even from miles away. When we first crossed paths at the motorcycle shop—during the early days of the all-female volunteer group I started—she was everything I admired in a woman: strong, independent, unafraid to take up space, and guided by a heart that always leaned toward kindness. Years later, life had shaped her into a devoted wife and mother, but that same fearless compassion still defined her. Courtney was rare in the way she loved people—steadfast, genuine, and without conditions. She was one of the few friends who ever treated me the way I treated my friends: like family. And when I found myself running for my life, there wasn't a moment of hesitation about who to call. It would be Courtney—because even from far away, she was home.

"Hello?" Her voice was groggy but instantly alert. "What's wrong?"

The sound of her voice brought tears to my eyes. Help was on the way.

"Courtney, I'm not safe," I said, my voice cracking under the weight of exhaustion and fear. "I don't even have the energy to explain everything right now, but I need somewhere safe to go with the girls."

She didn't hesitate. "Well, come on then! We've got plenty of room. We'll figure it all out together."

I choked back a sob. "Tray's lost it. I might be putting you in danger—"

"I said come on," she interrupted firmly. "You will be safe, loved, and have everything you need here. That's it."

Her certainty was like a lifeline. "Okay... okay," I whispered, my voice barely steady. "I guess we'll see you in about eight hours."

"Alright. I love you."

"I love you too."

The tears spilled over as I hung up. I didn't even have time to cry properly. I wiped my face and dialed the next number. I needed help.

My mom answered almost immediately, and I launched into it. "Mom, I need your help. I'm leaving town, but I can't do this alone, will you come with me? I don't know if I'll come back, but I promise I'll buy you a bus ticket to get back when you are ready."

"Okay, baby," she said softly. It was a short call; she didn't push for details, though I could hear the worry in her voice. Of course, she still had to ask, "Are you hungry?"

That was just like her. Even in a crisis, her love came through with simple questions like that.

Within the hour, we were all on the road, my mom, my six week old, my eight year old, and me heading for Louisiana.

When we arrived at Courtney's house, I was nothing more than a hollow shell, a ghost of myself. I had one baby in my arms and another holding my hand. The weight of it all threatened to crush me, but for the first time in days, I felt a flicker of hope.

We weren't safe yet, but we were on our way.

The first day was a haze. Courtney had set up her camper for us, giving me a little privacy. I slept. I was grateful my mom was there because she took over with Abbie, feeding her, changing her, doing all the things I just couldn't. I stayed in that bed, crying, sleeping, and searching for any courage to keep going. My body betrayed me every time Abbie cried, my breasts aching for her, but I couldn't move. It took two full days before I could leave that bed.

When I did, I wasn't free—I was still stuck in the cycle. I kept texting Tray, taking his calls. I wouldn't tell him where we were. Only my mom and Courtney knew. I'd pace up and down her driveway, phone in hand, begging him to go to rehab, asking him how he could choose drugs over us. I couldn't see it for what it was—abuse. I thought he was just sick, an addict, and if he could get help, we could still be a family.

The calls were a constant storm of emotions. He'd switch between love-bombing me, filling my head with promises of change, and threatening me, his voice laying out the well-made trap I was simply blind to. The moment he realized I wasn't coming back, he lashed out, demanding to know where we were; and when that didn't work, the threats would escalate. He told me more than once he'd kill me if I didn't come home.

I started going to Al-Anon meetings, searching for something—community, answers, peace. I spoke with officers, lawyers, and even an abuse shelter, trying to figure out what to do next. Every option felt impossible. A protection order would mean no contact for a month, but it also felt like giving up any chance to convince Tray to get help. Having him arrested? That wasn't something I could handle. Divorce? That didn't even cross my mind until Tray mentioned it, and then the lawyer's fees left me in shock.

I didn't want any of this. I just wanted the father of my children to get better. But it became clearer by the day that wasn't going to happen.

The summer wore on, and my girls played with Courtney's kids like nothing was wrong. Courtney had planned a Fourth of July party long before we arrived, and she went through with it. Everyone laughed and celebrated, but I was barely holding it together. When a bottle rocket backfired and scared Lillie, I broke. She was fine, but I wasn't. That was supposed to be a "dad job," I thought bitterly.

After the party, I tried to distract myself. I even took a waitressing job, but it left me feeling emptier than before.

One day, I went for a long drive, so consumed by everything that I almost didn't come back. I was unraveling, and Tray knew it. That's when his manipulations started to work.

He promised me everything. Rehab. Change. A fresh start. He said he just wanted to see the girls, and we could live with his mom while he got better. Against my better judgment, and despite Courtney and my mom begging me not to go, I gave in.

Courtney told me later she was sure that if I left, I wouldn't come back. She wasn't wrong to be scared. Leaving an abusive relationship is the most dangerous time.

It's not like in the movies. You don't just wake up with bruises and decide to leave. You love them, even when it's wrong. You believe in them. You need it to work.

So there I was, heading back to Georgia, clinging to the hope that Tray would keep his promises, even as my heart whispered I'd made a terrible mistake.

I thought we had a plan. Something fragile but full of hope. I would take the girls back to Georgia, live with his mother. He would go to rehab. We would all have space to heal. For once, I believed that maybe—just maybe—this cycle could be broken.

But all it took was one visit for the hope to shatter.

He pulled up like a storm, unannounced and boiling with rage. I watched him through the window—jaw clenched, fists tight at his sides, that look in his eyes I knew all too well. It wasn't sadness. It wasn't regret. It was control slipping through his fingers, and he was willing to burn it all down to get it back.

He didn't knock. He just started yelling—wild, accusatory, venom-laced words hurled like knives. "You're crazy! You think you can just take my kids?!" His voice, once familiar, now sounded like it came from a stranger—a monster wearing his skin.

In his hand, he held a keychain with a retractable wire, spinning it slowly, almost rhythmically. It was like he wanted me to wonder—what could he do with that? What *would* he do with that?

Every muscle in my body went tight, alert. My breath caught in my throat like it was afraid to move.

Then he charged.

"I'm taking them! I'm leaving with MY kids!"

I stepped in front of the door, legs trembling, arms out like a shield. I wasn't brave—I was desperate. Desperate to protect my babies, to buy them one more second of safety.

SLAM! His body collided with mine, and I was thrown back.

His arm pressed against my throat, not hard enough to crush it—just hard enough to let me know he *could.* My back hit the door with a dull thud, pain rippling through my spine. The pressure on my neck wasn't just physical—it was the weight of every time I'd ignored my instincts, every time I let love excuse the danger.

I fumbled for my phone, hands shaking, heart galloping, a scream stuck somewhere inside me that couldn't escape.

But he was faster. He ripped it from my hand and hurled it across the yard like it was nothing. Like *I* was nothing.

His mother screamed at him to stop. But her voice was static in the chaos.

Then he leaned in, voice low, words sliding into my ear like ice.

"You're lucky she's here," he hissed. "If she wasn't, I'd end you. Right here."

Time fractured.

I don't know how he got backed off. I don't remember how I made it inside. Just the slamming of the door, the frantic locking of every bolt with trembling fingers. No phone. No help. Just the deafening sound of my newborn crying and my own heart trying to beat its way out of my chest.

Inside, my oldest had seen everything through the window. Her tiny face was pale, eyes wide, too young to understand, too old to forget.

And still—why did I let him back in?

His mom begged me, "Just let him say goodbye to the kids." My mind screamed no, but my body moved anyway. I took the baby into the hallway and paced back and forth while I heard the mutters coming from the other room telling me the man who just attacked me was now inside the house.

I peeked around the corner to see Tray holding Lillie in his arms, tears streaming, but they weren't the tears of a father, they were the crocodile tears of a man manipulating his last scraps of power. He whispered poison in her ears, told her lies about me, rewrote the story before she was old enough to question the ending.

His mom found me in the hallway, gently took the baby from me, and Tray gave her a half-hearted goodbye; she was too young to manipulate.

And then he left.

I collapsed into a silence that only comes after a scream so loud your body gives up.

I sat there on the couch, baby crying in my arms, arms that felt too heavy to lift. My body was still. My soul wasn't. It felt like something inside me had split wide open—not broken but torn. Ripped apart by the sharp edge of betrayal, sorrow, and guilt.

There is a pain no one tells you about, the torment of surviving what you knew you should've escaped long ago. The pain of seeing your child's innocence get stripped by the very person you once trusted with your life. It's a hollow kind of ache. Not sharp, not loud. Just a dull, persistent void that lives in your chest, right where your hope used to be.

I texted my friend, Crystal, and asked if I could come for dinner. No details. Just a simple request. I needed to be near safety, near warmth, near someone who didn't look at me like I was broken.

Crystal is the mother of Julie, a friend of my daughters, and I knew she had been through a hell of her own. And when I finally told her what had happened, when I said the words out loud, gave them shape and breath, the weight of it all crushed me.

"Chelsea, you were just abused," Crystal said with deep concern in her voice.

I began to cry, my mind sobering up to the hard truth. *Oh my god, oh my god. She's right. This is what's happening. This is what abuse is. I can't do this. I can't be this mother. I won't be this mother.* I picked up the phone. With hands that still trembled, I called the police.

I wasn't brave. I was done being afraid.

That call was the beginning. Not the end of the nightmare, but the first real step toward waking up from it.

* * *

THE COURTHOUSE WAS COLD. THE KIND OF STERILE COLD that settles in your bones. I remember sitting in that waiting room, newborn bundled against my chest, Lillie coloring quietly beside me, too used to grown-up offices and tired eyes. I looked around at the other women—some with bruises still fresh, some holding back tears, some staring into space like they were still half inside the trauma—and I realized I wasn't alone. We were all different versions of the same story.

When I stood in front of the judge and explained why I needed a protection order, I could feel my voice shake. But I spoke anyway. I let the words fall, one by one—

evidence of what I had survived, of what I refused to live through again. This was the start of a long process: getting a protection order, moving out on my own, truly separating from him for good. And nothing about it was clean or easy or fast. Trauma doesn't let you walk in straight lines. It pulls at your ankles, whispers in your ear, makes you doubt your every decision.

Filing that paperwork, just putting pen to paper, felt like a betrayal of the years I'd spent believing he could change. But it also felt like I was writing the first page of a new life—one where fear didn't sleep beside me.

Moving out on my own was another kind of grief. Not because I missed him—but because I had to mourn the version of life I had hoped for. The dream of a whole family, of safety that never existed for me. I was choosing a harder road, one without certainty or comfort. But it was mine. And for the first time, I wasn't walking it in his shadow.

There were nights I sobbed into my pillow after the girls were asleep, overwhelmed by the weight of it all. Bills. Diapers. Court dates. Isolation. The lingering voice in my head that told me I'd fail, that I wasn't enough.

But each morning, I got up. I made breakfast. I kissed scraped knees. I sang lullabies. I called lawyers. I found rides. I kept going.

Because healing isn't loud. It's not dramatic or beautiful or cinematic. Sometimes it's just showing up—even when your hands are shaking. Even when your chest feels hollow.

I wasn't "over it." I wasn't healed. But I had chosen myself. I had chosen my daughters. And I would keep choosing us every single day.

This was the beginning of a new kind of hard. But it was also the beginning of my becoming.

Chapter Five

TWO HOURS BOTH WAYS

Healing: Crying, worry, bargaining, anger, accepting help, staring into space, having no voice, No. Having no words, no energy, blank.

Healing takes time.

Overthinking, overwhelmed, worried about others, no energy to worry about others, coming out of the nothingness.

Healing takes time.

Anger, confusion, why, knowing but yet not knowing, finding something to symbolize the process, sending help home, looking closer to home for routine.

Healing takes time.

Going through the motions, one foot in front of the other, bite size pieces, hyper sense of awareness: They noticed I smiled/they noticed I'm not talking as much/ they notice...

Healing takes time.

Making plans for the future, unsure of the future, getting exhausted quickly, spending time with family, unable to talk to friends, anger, sadness, appreciation for my life, the little things, the big things, a smile...

Healing takes time.

Back to routine. What is routine, what was my routine going to be, should be, should have been. What is the point of routine?

Healing takes time.

Work, home, dinner, mother. How to do these things. Auto pilot: I know how. I do these things.

Healing takes time.

Mindset is everything. This time I won't... This time we will... We are good. I am great, thanks for asking! I can do this.

Healing takes time.

Eating emotions; it's just a soda, it's just ice cream, fast food is just easier. One glass of wine is normal.

Healing takes time.

The cracks start to show. A bottle of wine is fine. A little fight is fine. A messy house is fine. It's fine. I'm fine.

Healing takes time.

More wine, more tears, more fears. Trying new things, meditation, journaling, support groups.

Healing takes time.

It's not fine! You are not fine! Life yells it. Pain both emotional and somehow physical escalates, all of it is bad. None of it was ever fine. What is the point? What is the purpose? What are we doing in life? What is life?

Healing takes time.

ANGER… Alone… Empty… Lost.
Healing takes time.
WHY?! Why did this happen? Why me? What did I do? I'm sorry! Why am I fighting with the people I love? Why do I hurt? Why me? Why us? Why?!
Healing takes time.
Support. Family. Friends. Have they been here the whole time?
Healing takes time.
Two months, it's not been as long as it feels. Self-imposed time line shattered, next step… Therapy. Medicine maybe? Anxiety, panic attacks. Put away the wine. Going through the motions of what should help. Will it help? Gym, meditation, books, talking, opening up, eating healthier, journaling.
Healing takes time.

Finding myself with nothing and two babies to care for was a reality I never imagined. With no home to call my own, I had to start over from scratch. It's funny, when I was bouncing from one friend's couch to another, I didn't even realize I was "homeless." Survival mode blinds you to the bigger picture. It wasn't until later that the weight of it all hit me.

In those early days, survival looked like leaning on the women who stepped in without hesitation. When I first began the process of obtaining a restraining order, we spent about a week staying at my friend Crystal's house. I was in hiding then, careful about who knew our location, terrified that Tray might find us and hurt us. Crystal didn't ask questions or expect explanations—she simply opened her door. She gave my children and me clothes to wear, beds to sleep in, and a sense of safety when everything felt uncertain. In her home, we were more than a burden or a crisis; we were cared for.

Not long after, we moved in with my friend Tanya. Her husband was a police officer, and we believed it would be safer there. Tanya and her family took us in completely, feeding us, giving us beds, and surrounding my girls with normalcy through play and routine. Her daughter played with mine as if nothing was wrong, and in those moments, my children were just kids again. When it came time to move into our new place, Tanya was there, helping us haul what little we had and making sure we didn't walk into that next chapter empty-handed. Between her and other friends, our bare space slowly filled: dishes, forks, cups, shampoo, laundry soap, bedding, proof that starting over didn't have to mean starting alone. It truly took a village to rebuild our lives, and those women carried us when I didn't yet know how to carry myself.

Two days after school started, I found what would become our home: a small, rundown single-wide trailer in a one-stoplight town, just ten minutes from my mom's place. It wasn't much, but it was ours.

Mom's unwavering support made it all possible. She stepped in to care for both my newborn and older child while I went back to work, offering me the chance to begin building something better for us, something that didn't carry the weight of what we'd lived through. Leaving behind the life we had known for so long was bitter, but there was no room for sentiment. There was no time to mourn what we were leaving behind. We had to move forward.

The court-ordered date came to collect what was left of our belongings from my old home, and I knew it was going to be chaotic. My village—my closest friends and family—showed up. They came ready to help, armed with black trash bags, their eyes set on getting this done. We rented a U-Haul, understanding the pressure of time. The police had given us just 30 minutes to clear out the girls' rooms and grab whatever I could salvage.

When we arrived, reality hit me like a ton of bricks. The house felt like a hollow shell. What had once been "mine" was gone—clothes, shoes, even the small treasures I had kept since childhood; along with the crib, baby swing, and a special gift my mom had made for the baby, the custom rocking horse she'd carefully crafted—gone. My mind went blank, as if someone had flipped a switch. The ground beneath me felt like it had dropped away, and all I could do was stand there, disoriented, unable to do anything. I wandered around in circles, my voice a whisper as I repeated the same question over and over, "How? Why?"

But no answers came. No clarity. Just the cold weight of the loss. I couldn't even bring myself to pack anything. It was like I had been paralyzed by the reality of what was happening. I was on autopilot, feeling like a stranger in a place that had once been my home.

And then I saw him. Standing in the doorway, his eyes locked onto mine with a dark, almost hollow intensity. It had been a month since we spoke and maybe two since I'd seen him. His gaze pierced through me, like it could see straight into my soul. His pupils were dilated, his face drawn and pale from whatever he'd been using. He was high—high and dangerous. But the way he stood there, that cocky, evil smile twisting at the corners of his lips, I knew he felt nothing but pride in the destruction he'd caused. He knew. He knew exactly what he'd done to me, to us.

He didn't need to say anything. His eyes alone—those dark, cold eyes—spoke volumes. The contempt, the cruelty, the satisfaction he took in my pain—it all radiated from him like a dark cloud. My heart raced, and for a split second, I was frozen. All I could do was stare back at him, too terrified to move, too stunned to speak.

But then I heard the officer's voice behind me, cutting through the thick tension. "We need to keep it moving," he said, his tone firm but measured. The officer positioned himself between me and my ex, his body a clear barrier, and I realized, with a jolt, that the only thing separating me from him now—the only thing keeping me safe—was the badge and the uniform of the police officer standing between us.

I didn't know how long I stood there, my body stiff, my mind spinning. All I could feel was the weight of his stare, like he was daring me to do something, anything, that would give him an excuse to finish what he'd started all those years ago. But I couldn't move. I didn't trust myself. I didn't trust him. Leaving an abusive partner is the most dangerous time for a victim. Studies show that women are 70 times more likely to be killed in the weeks after leaving than at any other time during the relationship.

Thankfully, my village didn't wait for me to snap out of it—they stepped in, started moving, and got to work. They didn't need me to ask for help; they just gave it. As they loaded up the U-Haul, it wasn't my things filling the trailer, but mostly Lillie's—her books, her toys, her clothes. And as small as that victory felt in the grand scheme of things, I clung to it with everything I had. At least she had her things. At least I was doing something right for her.

Among the things packed up was her giant stuffed rainbow caterpillar. It had been with her for as long as I could remember—its colorful, plush body a comfort to her after the chaos and unpredictability we had lived through. It had always been by her side, a quiet constant in a world full of upheaval. But somehow, in all the turmoil of the past weeks, it had gone missing. She had asked for it every day, and every day, I had to tell her I couldn't find it.

Now, seeing it sitting there in the U-Haul, its rainbow body bright against the dark backdrop of the trailer, something inside me softened. My heart lifted. She was going to have it back. She was going to get that piece of comfort, that thing she had clung to through all of this. I was able to make it right, at least this one thing. It felt like a victory, a small win in a world where everything had felt so defeated.

As we pulled out of the driveway I noticed a large burn pile still smoking. That was the moment I knew exactly what had happened to all of the "missing" items. Later confirmed by others, he had indeed burned it all. However, that smile—Lillie's big, bright smile—was worth more than anything else I had lost. It reminded me that, despite everything, we were still okay. We would be okay.

Standing there, in the middle of that run-down, single-wide trailer with its faded walls and peeling wallpaper, I couldn't help but think about my mom. This was what she had gone through—what she had lived through all those years. This was how she ended up in the same kind of place I now found myself, the same kind of home I had grown up in. But I wasn't going to give up, not now, not when I had my girls to care for. I wasn't going to let history repeat itself.

Determined to make it work, I turned the small living room into a makeshift nursery. It wasn't pretty, and it wasn't what I had dreamed of for my children, but it was what we had. Thanks to the generosity of friends and family, we made do with what we could find—mostly hand-me-downs, some old furniture, and whatever toys Lillie had outgrown. We didn't have much, but we had each other. And somehow, that was enough.

* * *

IN MY OLD LIFE, STRUCTURE WASN'T FREEDOM; IT WAS control. I measured my words carefully, adjusting my tone and expression to avoid setting off another storm. The placement of objects in the house, the timing of meals, even the silence between conversations held the potential for conflict. It was exhausting, living within a schedule not of my own making, but one dictated by fear and manipulation.

Structure carries a different weight now. It's almost ironic how before leaving, I thought of it as something beneficial, something that helped my family thrive. I began to understand that the structure I lived within was nothing more than walking on eggshells. It wasn't about balance or stability—it was about survival. Every action, from cooking to cleaning, even the way I spoke, was woven with triggers.

When I finally broke free, I thought I could leave that structure behind, but I quickly realized how deeply ingrained it was. At first, I tried to embrace chaos, to let go of the rigidity that had once defined my existence. But chaos didn't bring peace—it only amplified my anxiety.

Without realizing it, I had been conditioned to believe that if things weren't structured a certain way, disaster would follow.

Healing meant redefining structure. It meant creating routines that nurtured rather than oppressed. It meant finding safety in predictability, but on my own terms. I began to reclaim my space, allowing myself the grace to make choices that weren't based on fear or someone else's expectations. I learned to recognize my own triggers and separate them from reality.

One of the first ways I did this was by transforming our home into something that felt like *ours*. Bright yellows and pinks splashed across the walls, soft floral curtains, and cozy blankets in every shade of girlhood I had once been denied. If it was going to be just us girls, then I wanted our space to feel joyful, unapologetically feminine, a place where we could be soft, where we could breathe.

With our home reflecting warmth, I built a routine that gave me the stability I had craved for so long. Up at 5 a.m., the quiet hours before the world stirred became my time. I'd get the girls ready, drop them off, then head to my favorite coffee shop, letting the scent of espresso and the hum of early morning conversation ground me before the workday began. After work, I picked up the girls, we ate dinner together, sometimes something home-cooked, sometimes just whatever made us feel full. Then came bath time, bedtime, and finally, a moment of stillness.

For the first time in my life, structure didn't feel like a cage; it was freedom.

Everything that happened in my life had led me to this moment. And while the journey had been painful, I was learning that I could build a life with structure that served me—not one that caged me. Yin and yang, light and dark. I saw that true balance was not about eliminating the bad but learning how to rise from it.

One night, after what felt like an endless day of trying to juggle everything, I found myself at the store, standing in the aisle with my mind spinning. Tray had hidden the baby swing—just like he had hidden so many things, things that were mine, things that were meant for my children. I couldn't stand the thought of Abbie not having a swing, of her missing out on something so simple, something that would make her feel comforted.

So, I stood there in the store, the exhaustion heavy in my bones, but I pushed it down. I picked out a swing, looked at the price, and paid for it with the money I had earned from working long hours. It wasn't much, but it was mine. It was Abbie's.

When I got home, the house was quiet, and the girls were already asleep. Mom was getting ready to leave for the night, and we exchanged our usual promises of, "I'll see you tomorrow." I stayed behind, staring at the swing in the box, knowing I had a task ahead of me. I knew I couldn't just leave it there. I stayed up into the early hours, assembling it piece by piece, my body heavy with fatigue, but my heart full of a quiet, steady determination.

I didn't stop for anything—except when Abbie needed a bottle, of course. But once I had her fed, I went back to work. When I finally finished, when the swing was assembled and standing in the corner of the room, I stepped back. I felt something I hadn't allowed myself to feel: pride. I had done this. I had bought the swing with my own money and built it with my own hands. No one had helped me do it. I did it on my own.

Sitting there, in the dim light of the living room, watching the swing sway gently, I thought to myself: *Maybe I can do this. Maybe I really can do this alone.*

The idea didn't scare me. It gave me strength.

Chapter Six

CAREFULLY CRAFTED

Getting back into marketing felt like reclaiming a piece of myself I had been forced to leave behind. For years, I had worked as an accountant at an all-female firm, not because I loved it, but because it was the only career my ex would allow me to have. It was safe, predictable, and utterly devoid of the creative spark that once made me feel alive.

Then came Maja.

She was the kind of woman who exuded poised power, someone who didn't just see potential; she nurtured it. When I walked into that interview, nervous but determined, she saw past the years I had spent buried in numbers and restrictions.

"I know you've been out of marketing for a while," she said, leaning forward with a knowing look, "but that doesn't mean you've forgotten how to do it. Tell me—if I hired you today, what's the first thing you'd change about our current strategy?"

I answered without hesitation, and by the time I left that office, I knew something had shifted.

When she offered me the job, it felt like someone had cracked open a window in a room I hadn't realized was suffocating me.

The pay was better, yes, but more than that it was a fresh start. I was back in a field I loved, working in the heart of the city, surrounded by a team that challenged and inspired me. No longer trapped in a role that had been chosen for me, I was finally choosing for myself.

And Maja? She became more than a boss. She became a mentor, a friend, and a woman who reminded me what was possible when I stopped letting fear dictate my future.

That chance she took on me didn't just change my job, it changed the entire trajectory of my life.

The days were grueling however.

I commuted two hours each way into the city for this career, starting my mornings at 5 a.m. and finishing my days long after 7:50 p.m. when I picked up my kids from Mom's. Often, the only meals I had were ones she cooked for the babies while she waited for me to arrive. The nights were the hardest. After the kids were asleep, I would lie awake, staring at the ceiling, crying quietly as I wrestled with the enormity of our situation.

But even in those moments of despair, one thing kept me going: *My mother's story ended in a run-down single-wide, but mine won't.*

Healing from grooming and abuse was a long and

arduous process. It involved unlearning the fear and hyper-awareness that had become second nature. My body, influenced by the trauma, reacted with hormonal imbalances and physical manifestations of my emotions. Panic attacks, anxiety, and a constant state of alert were daily battles.

When I tried to stop the pain, I often ended up creating more. In an effort to protect myself, I became overly cautious, mistrustful, and isolated. I had to learn to distinguish between real threats and remnants of past fears.

Mornings became my sanctuary. After dropping off the girls, before the emails started flooding in, before the weight of the day settled onto my shoulders, I carved out space just for me. It wasn't much, just a quiet drive to the coffee shop, the world still wrapped in that soft, early-morning haze. But it was mine.

I would park in the same corner spot, step inside, and let the warmth and scent of freshly brewed coffee settle something deep in my chest. Some mornings, I'd bring a book, though I rarely turned the pages. Other mornings, I'd sit with my journal, trying to put words to the thoughts that felt too tangled to say out loud. And sometimes, I just sat, hands wrapped around my cup, staring out the window, breathing.

It wasn't about the coffee, really. It was about finding myself in the silence.

For most of my life, I had been an extension of

someone else, someone's wife, someone's mother, someone's employee. And before that, I was someone's victim. Every part of me had been shaped by survival, by making it through one more day, one more fight, one more impossible moment. But now, as I sat in that coffee shop with no one needing anything from me, I was finally asking myself the question I had been too afraid to face: Who am I when no one else is watching?

At first, I didn't have an answer.

I had spent so much time shrinking, bending, molding myself into what I thought I had to be that I wasn't sure what was left when I peeled all of that away. But morning after morning, sip after sip, I started to see her—the girl I used to be before the world got to her. The woman I wanted to become.

Not just an ex-wife. Not just a survivor. Not just a mother.

Chelsea.

She just needed to be known.

All areas of myself were tainted by the pain of what I'd been through. I had gone from being a soft, happy-go-lucky person to a hollow shell, and then into something even harder—a cold, unfeeling rock completely shut off from real emotions. I played my roles as a mother and employee like a starlet performing on stage, but inside, I was seething. I was angry. Angry at myself for ending up here. Angry at my appearance, at the way I spoke, at how small my dreams had been. But something shifted in that anger. It became fuel, igniting a fire deep within me to rediscover who I was.

Every time I looked in the mirror, I saw a stranger staring back. My friend had given me a few outfits to wear to work, but my closet was otherwise nearly empty, Tray had burned all my clothes. One weekend, while staring at the few pieces I owned, I remembered I had a credit card for Belk. *Why not?* It was time to do something for myself.

Walking into that store, I felt a mix of nerves and excitement. I headed straight for the sales rack, determined to stretch every dollar. In the dressing room, it felt like I was playing a scene straight out of a teen movie—trying on outfit after outfit, experimenting with styles, searching for something that felt like *me*. When I finally found the right pieces, I felt a little spark.

But I wasn't done yet. For years, I'd wanted to dye my hair jet black. I loved the idea of it, but Tray had always hated the thought, so I never did. Not anymore. I went to the salon and told the stylist exactly what I wanted. When she spun me around to face the mirror, I barely recognized myself, but I liked what I saw.

There I was, staring back at myself. It felt like meeting an old friend after years of being apart.

I'll never forget the pride I felt walking into work that Monday morning—bold black hair, a red dress hugging my frame, and a red lip to match. Red has always been my color. A statement. A declaration. A battle cry. It made me feel powerful, like I could take on the world. But more than that, it made me feel like I was alive again. Not just existing. Not just surviving. Alive.

That fire, once fueled by anger and pain, was changing. It wasn't just destruction anymore; it was transformation. It was becoming hope. It was becoming me.

And fiery, I was. That fire didn't just push me forward—it *catapulted* me into the next stage of my life. It wasn't just about faking it until I made it. No, I had to *face* it until I made it. And so, I did.

It wasn't overnight. Some days felt like progress, others like drowning.

* * *

Eyes open. A new day. Is it Saturday? Yes, it's Saturday. Mom has the kids. But there is no sudden awakening, no cinematic gasp for air. Just the slow, sinking weight of reality pressing in—like standing at the edge of the ocean, waves washing over my feet, pulling me deeper into the wet, grainy sand. How could I go from feeling invincible one moment to hollow the next?

I'd reach for my phone, desperate for an escape. Maybe a text, maybe a call. Something to pull me out of my head. Social media became a blur of artificial highs and suffocating lows—happy lives I didn't believe in, despairing ones that mirrored my own. An endless cycle of comparison, an algorithm that somehow knew exactly what I was feeling. Switch app. Scroll. Switch app. Close app.

A message buzzed through the static. A friend.

"Why am I so messed up?"

I laughed to myself. Maybe I'm not the only one to ask that today…

The conversation flickered between shared confessions and empty reassurances—like a game of tennis where no one really wins. Eventually, I hit a wall. My chest tightened, my head spun, and before I could stop it, I pulled the comforter over my head. I needed to disappear for a while.

Sleep came, but it wasn't rest. It was drifting into nothingness—an awareness of absence, like floating in a void with no edges, no gravity. My mind searched for meaning, for answers, for anything, but all I found were more questions.

I woke up, but I wasn't really awake. It was 12:30 p.m., and I felt sticky with sweat. Gross. Heavy. Empty. Snap out of it.

I reached for human connection again, desperate for an anchor. Oh, desperation—my toxic companion. Was it a weakness? A strength? Who was I without it? Overthinking. Stop.

Text sent. Feet on the floor. Get dressed. Brush teeth. Nothing.

I pinpointed the feeling. Loneliness. Unseen. And the worst part? I was the architect of my own isolation.

That realization pulled me under again. I gave in. Fuck it.

I craved three things: chocolate, validation, praise. In theory, none of these were inherently bad. But the way I clung to them, consumed them—like they could fill the aching void inside me—made them poisonous. They rotted me from the inside out, slowly and unforgivingly. I needed the rush. The high.

Validate my feelings, I plead with my friend. Praise my existence, I tease my fuck toy, consumption of unhealthy food and behavior filling the emptiness for a few hours... And for a few hours, I felt something. Anything.

And then, just as quickly, the high faded. The cycle started again. I cleaned, rearranged, distracted myself from the chaos within by controlling the space around me. My mom dropped off the kids. Evening routines followed. Dinner. Bedtime. Soft, fleeting moments that reminded me I was capable of love came from the forgiving eyes of my children.

But when night fell, the loneliness returned. The ache of being unseen.

Lying in bed, I reached for my phone one last time. A video flickered across the screen, whispering of release, of letting go, of healing. One final text—maybe to remind myself, maybe to remind my friend from earlier in the day—and I closed my eyes.

Tomorrow would bring a restart button.

* * *

THERAPY WAS CRUCIAL IN THIS JOURNEY. IT GAVE ME A SAFE space to unravel the layers of trauma, to *name* the wounds, to understand the patterns. My therapist helped me recognize the cycle of abuse, the enablers, the grief that came in waves. I learned to identify trauma responses—not just in myself, but in my children, in the people around me.

Awareness became my armor:

- Knowing to get out of the car and lock the door behind me.
- Keeping my phone charged and staying alert to my surroundings.
- Avoiding alcohol to keep my mind sharp in case of emergencies.
- Keeping a go-bag packed with essentials.
- Printing out important documents and placing them in safe hands.

It was exhausting. But it was necessary.

Because survival wasn't just about leaving, it was about rebuilding. About finding my way back to myself.

It meant returning to work with my head held high, wearing red. It meant learning to embrace love again, not as a crutch, but as a conscious, powerful choice. It meant standing in front of the mirror, looking at the scars, and realizing they didn't define me. They were just marks from a battle I had survived. They told the story of a woman who fought and kept going.

It meant knowing, deep in my bones, that I was still here. Still rising. And I wasn't done yet, and I wasn't alone.

The very same friends I thought I had lost during my marriage became my lifeline. They showed up in ways I never expected, in ways that reminded me I wasn't alone. They invited us over for dinners when the loneliness felt unbearable. They helped clean the house when exhaustion threatened to consume me. They watched the girls when I couldn't be there, giving me space to rebuild a life that had once felt impossible.

The guilt of being away from my daughters gnawed at me, whispering that I should be doing more, that I should be better. But I reminded myself, this was temporary. This struggle, this in-between, was the path to something better. And step by step, I was getting there.

I remember one particular day, after a long morning at work, I had a therapy appointment. I clocked out for lunch and slid into my car, heart racing a little at the thought of the conversation that lay ahead. I clicked on the Zoom link, adjusted my rearview mirror, and tried to breathe deeply as the connection loaded.

"Hello, Chelsea," my therapist's voice came through, warm and calm. "Where should we start today?"

Doctor Monroe, who specialized in relationship

trauma, was a tall, thin woman with moussie brown hair and soft brown eyes that exuded peace and compassion. I looked forward to my calls with her, as they were a lifeline to me during such a tumultuous time.

I crossed my arms, gripping the sleeves of my sweater, but it did nothing to ground me. The tension sat heavy in my chest, pressing against my ribs like a vice.

My therapist tilted her head slightly, watching me with that patient, knowing expression. "You look tense today. What's on your mind?"

I let out a sharp breath, my fingers digging into the fabric of my jeans. "I heard he has someone new."

She didn't react, didn't flinch or look surprised. She just nodded, waiting. "And how does that make you feel?"

A bitter laugh slipped out before I could stop it. "Angry. Sad. Relieved that it's not me anymore. But mostly…" I swallowed, my throat tight. "Mostly, I feel sick. Like I can see it all happening again, like I'm watching her walk right into the same trap I barely crawled out of."

Her voice was gentle, but steady. "That's a normal response. Your brain is recognizing the patterns, the danger. It's a trigger because it reminds you of your own experience."

I clenched my jaw. "But I can't do anything. I want to shake her, warn her, tell her to run—but I know she won't listen." I hesitated, the truth pressing against my ribs. "I wouldn't have."

Silence stretched between us for a moment before she

spoke again. "You can't save her, Chelsea." Her words weren't cruel, just honest. "But you can keep healing. You can remind yourself that you got out. And maybe, one day, she will too."

I let out a sigh, feeling the weight of all the thoughts swirling in my head. "I don't know," I said, almost frustrated with myself. "I just feel like... I haven't made much progress. I feel stuck. Like I'm standing still, not getting anywhere."

"Well," she replied, her tone thoughtful, "Let's review the things you've overcome then."

I stared out the windshield for a moment, trying to collect my thoughts, and then it spilled out. "I left, I'm living on my own now... I've got this new career that feels real, and I've found a place to rent, something stable. I've been able to make my own decisions, choose what's best for me."

I paused, the weight of those words settling on me. It was true. But somehow, it didn't feel like enough.

My therapist waited, giving me space to think. Then, with a kind yet firm tone, she said, "Chelsea, you've been doing all of that on the outside, but do you realize what a big step that is? Most of my clients start with the internal work—the healing, the self-discovery—and then work their way outward. But you... you discovered the person you wanted to be and began living that on the outside first. You shifted your perspective, your environment, your actions. Now you're working on the inside, bringing that alignment between who you are and who you want to be."

I was silent for a long moment, processing what she'd just said. I hadn't thought about it that way before. In the chaos of rebuilding, in all the things I was doing, I had never stopped to consider that the biggest change—the most important one—was already happening on the outside. The shift had already started, and it was all part of the bigger journey.

It was huge.

Now, I just had to give myself the grace to let the inside catch up.

"I never thought of it that way," I said softly, a quiet awe in my voice. "I thought the healing had to start with the inside, and everything else would follow. But... I guess I've been doing it the other way around."

"You've been doing it in your own way," she said gently, "and that's okay. The truth is, there's no one right way to heal. It's just about moving forward, no matter how that looks. And, Chelsea, you're doing it. You're showing up for yourself every day, and that's more than many people ever do."

I sat in that car for a while longer after we said our goodbyes, feeling the weight of her words sink in. I had been showing up. Even when I didn't feel like I could. Even when my body felt heavy with the scars of my past. I had walked back into work, into life, with my head held high, when it was the hardest thing to do. And I was still doing it.

The truth was, I wasn't stuck. I was simply in the middle of something. Something I hadn't fully understood yet. But I was moving forward. Maybe not in the way I had imagined, maybe not as fast as I wanted, but I was moving. And for now, that was enough.

Chapter Seven

BEHIND CLOSED DOORS

As I started to remove my clothing from the day, I tried to focus on the sound of the running shower and less on the garments that fell to the floor. Each piece of fabric felt tainted. Dirty from the news I heard that day, dirty from the past that is still haunting me. Dirty in the literal sense too, considering I had started my period and sat in a puddle of my own blood most of the day.

I couldn't help but let my mind spin around the strange symbolism of it all. Maybe I wanted to feel filthy. I already felt it on the inside. I felt it crawling across my skin. I felt it rising off of me and filling the room, reaching the noses of the people I stood a little too close to today. I didn't want their advice, their hugs, or their apologies. Maybe that is why I didn't go home and change. Either way, I wanted it all off of me now. I wanted a fresh start.

Fresh start. Fresh start.

It sounded beautiful. I thought I had that. I built a whole new life. Then the past came knocking once again.

I don't think I will ever forget my friend's face when she realized the severity of what I had lived through. How could she know? She was part of my carefully crafted new life. She wasn't there when I was broken. She wasn't there when I picked up one of those shattered pieces of myself and finally fought back.

Her eyes reflected the smallest fragment of my pain, placed before me like a mirror.

I let my mind finally absorb the news. It came through a quiet phone call from a concerned acquaintance. My ex was back in jail. He had strangled another woman. He had another victim and as the details came to light all I could see was 17-year-old Chelsea.

I folded into myself as the truth settled in, the unbearable knowing that I couldn't save her, or the next woman, or the one after that. Shit, I questioned if I had really even saved myself as dirty as I felt. I had tried to warn her, but from where I stood in her life, my words never carried far enough.

I splashed water on my face. This was the shower I had been waiting on all day.

I took the bar of soap and washed. I rushed through it because I felt dirty. I wondered if anyone else has ever felt this way. I even washed between each toe before abruptly getting out.

None of my clothes felt right.

I didn't feel right.

I felt tainted by the day and the news I had received.

Sexuality is a topic that often feels like it's locked behind closed doors, something we're taught to keep quiet about, to tuck away neatly where it won't make anyone uncomfortable. But the truth? It's not separate from us. It weaves itself into our lives in ways we don't always recognize; shaped by our experiences, our traumas, and our healing.

We have to talk about the things that hurt if we ever want to heal from them. We have to address the elephant in the room; the way trauma tangles itself into the way we see ourselves, the way we love, the way we desire. I remember a time even after I had accepted I was an abuse survivor that I couldn't admit I was sexually abused. Because, well, I had consented, right? However, I came to find that "consent" is a much more complex word.

For twelve years, I was his. Not in the way love binds two people together, but in the way ownership sinks into your bones, making you forget where you end and he begins. This didn't go away overnight. I was 16 when we met, 19 when we married; too young to know what forever should feel like, too naive to understand saying "I do" wouldn't make me safe, wouldn't make me loved. He was 23, a man by the world's standards, though I now know real men don't need to break something to feel powerful.

For a decade, he decided everything—what I wore, who I spoke to, how I saw myself. He carved me into someone small, someone easy to control. And when I finally left, when I walked away with nothing but my name and the weight of all he had done, the silence was unbearable.

After years of surviving, of walking on eggshells, of knowing exactly how to move to keep him from snapping, I didn't know what to do with myself. I didn't know who I was without his voice drowning out my own. And worst of all, I still wanted him. It was a mental state precipitated by sexual trauma. So my mind would think in ways I was conditioned to think for almost a decade. I thought the only way to please my partner was doing every twisted fantasy he wanted; to play the role of a pornstar. To perform, doing whatever "he needed" and disregarding any natural warning signs my body had to protect me.

I hated him. I knew what he had done. I knew how he twisted love into something ugly, something painful. But my body had learned to crave him, to respond to his hands even when my mind screamed *NO*. I hated that some nights, I still imagined his touch, my skin still burned with the memory of him. I wanted him to tell me what to do. To inflict pain, whether that was calling me a slut or bruising my body.

I'm ashamed to admit I went back to him twice, and after the second time I was physically ill.

How do you untangle desire, unwind the betrayal of your own body's sexual longings leading you into destructive behaviors? I didn't ask for this but now here I was with a rewired brain, and I was no electrician. How do you separate what was real from what was forced?

It had never mattered before. My wants, my desires— they were never part of the equation. I was taught to surrender, to let him take. Now, standing in the wreckage of my past, I wasn't sure what was left of me. I didn't know if I had ever truly wanted him, or if I had just accepted he was the only choice I had.

Some nights, I let myself wonder, let myself dream. Of soft hands. Of lips that didn't press hard enough to bruise. Of a love that didn't come with fear. I didn't have the answers yet, but I was finally asking the questions.

And maybe, just maybe, that was the first step to stopping the cycle.

Leaving Tray wasn't about walking out of a house, it was stepping into the unknown. My life wasn't dictated by his moods, his wants, his control anymore. It was just me.

I was both exhilarated and terrified.

The silence in my new place felt different. It wasn't tense, and I wasn't anticipating the next explosion. It was empty in a way that made my stomach twist. How to just *be,* escaped my grasp. Who was I outside of the girl who had spent her entire adult life keeping a man like him happy just to stay safe?

That's when Mom showed up one afternoon, holding a bottle of cheap moscato like she was about to fix everything with a screw top.

"Alright," she said, plopping down next to me on the warped trailer's porch with an energy that felt almost giddy. She lit a Virginia slim and blew out the smoke. "You're single," she said in her raspy voice, determined to shake things up. "It's time we do something about that."

I laughed, shaking my head. "Mom, I just left my marriage. Maybe dating isn't exactly—"

She waved me off, already reaching for my phone. Then she stopped and turned to me, looking over her Dollar Store readers, and shot me the look. The look that said you-don't-have-a-choice-here. "You don't have to *date* anyone," she said. "But you do have to remember there's a whole world out there. And you're allowed to want things for yourself."

I sighed, but deep down, I knew she was right. I had spent so many years believing my body, my desires, my choices belonged to someone else. I wasn't even sure what I liked, what I wanted. But I knew I wanted to find out.

So, with a full glass of wine and my mom giggling like a teenager, we downloaded the app. It felt ridiculous and surreal, swiping through strangers like shopping for shoes. She helped me pick out pictures, the ones where I looked happy, where I looked like *me*—whoever that was.

At first, it was just a joke. Even my profile read something humorous. Then I met someone who caught my vixen side's attention. A bottle of wine later and things hit hyper speed. The texting filled every free moment I had for a solid week, then it graduated to more.

A one-night stand, something I told myself was just a way to reclaim my body, to prove to myself that I was in control now. It wasn't about love. It wasn't even about connection. It was about power—about stepping into something that had been stolen from me for years.

The first time I did it, I felt reckless and alive; the kind of alive that comes from doing something you shouldn't. My hands shook as I got dressed afterward, heart pounding as I walked out of that stranger's apartment, still tasting the thrill of being wanted, of being seen as something more than a possession. I thought I would feel shame. I thought I would regret it. Instead, I felt electric.

That one night turned into another version of a meaningless fling. And then another. Soon, it wasn't just the act; it was the chase, the rush of flirtation that started long before hands ever touched. It was the way men looked at me, the way they told me I was sexy, that they wanted me, that I was *desirable*. I wasn't Tray's wife anymore. I wasn't just a girl who had spent a decade shrinking into someone else's shadow. I was someone who could make men hunger with just a few words on a screen.

The dating app became my playground, my battlefield, my therapy. I learned how to tease, how to dangle myself just enough to keep them coming back. I learned how to be a fantasy, how to wield my body like a weapon. With each interaction, I felt more like a woman in control, more like someone who had taken back what was hers.

But there were parts of me I couldn't get back. Pieces I

gave away too freely, not realizing until later how much I had lost. Late at night, when the phone screen went dark, I was still alone. The rush faded. The messages slowed. And I was left wondering if I had reclaimed something or if I had just found a new way to lose myself.

The high never lasted. No matter how many flirty messages I sent or how many men whispered that I was irresistible, it was never enough. The thrill burned fast and bright, but the emptiness crept in just as quickly. It was like drinking salt water, momentarily satisfying but leaving me thirstier than before. I wanted more—*needed* more.

The truth was, the men on the apps weren't giving me what my deep subconscious mind and my body really craved. They didn't *know* my pain. They didn't see the parts of me that had been shaped by a decade of Tray's control. The way he had rewired my body and mind, blurring the lines between pain and pleasure, love and obedience. The way his touch had made me feel *owned*, and how, for reasons I still couldn't fully explain, a part of me missed that.

Tray had introduced me to the *kink* scene early in our marriage. At first, I thought it was just another way for us to connect. It seemed for him, however, it was just another way to control me. I, like most, also thought it was going to be like Fifty Shades of Gray. I would be chained and whipped and told what to do. In ways, yes, the twisted form of the craft he presented to me was exactly that. But in the rare moments when it was about more than just *him*, when I let myself sink into the surrender, something inside me *clicked*. There was a structure, a clarity in those moments that the chaos of our relationship lacked. And now, out in the world on my own, grasping for something that would make me feel whole again, I thought maybe that was the answer.

So I went searching. For what exactly, that part I was still figuring out.

I scrolled through new profiles with terms I barely understood, looking for someone who could pull me out of the spiral, who could give me what Tray once had. Only this time without the cruelty, without the fear. I told myself this was about healing, about reclaiming that part of myself, about erasing his touch from every inch of me, about proving that I could separate the pleasure from the past.

But deep down, I knew the truth.

I was scared that healing my sexual trauma wasn't in the cards for me. That my destiny was to be broken forever.

* * *

I FOUND HIM THE WAY I FOUND MOST OF THEM, THROUGH A carefully crafted profile on an app where people didn't have to pretend to be anything other than what they craved.

His username was simple, direct. No gimmicks, no unnecessary bravado. Just one word that hinted at authority without demanding it. His profile picture was subtle—no face, just the edge of a strong jawline, a dark suit, a hand resting casually on a desk. It was enough to make my stomach tighten with anticipation.

His first message wasn't like the others. No corny dominance clichés, no immediate demands. Just:

"What are you looking for?"

Not *who*—but *what*. It was the first time someone had asked me that outright. And for the first time, I hesitated. Because I wasn't sure I knew the answer.

I typed out something half-honest, half-guarded. *"Exploring. New to the lifestyle, but curious."*

His reply came quickly. *"Curious is good. Curious means you're thinking. Thinking means you're not just chasing a feeling—you want to be understood and to understand."*

It was such a simple response, but it hit differently. I was chasing something, but I hadn't admitted to myself what it was. Validation? Freedom? A way to reclaim my body after years of it not feeling like my own? Maybe all of it.

His name was Daniel, and we talked for months before I agreed to meet him. I even spoke to my therapist about it.

I sat on the couch, crossing my legs and then uncrossing them, unsure of how to start. My therapist, Dr. Monroe, waited patiently, her expression open and warm. She always knew when to let the silence hold space for me.

"I've been thinking a lot about my body," I finally said, exhaling as if the words had been stuck in my chest. "And how, for so long, it hasn't really felt like mine."

Dr. Monroe nodded. "That makes sense. After trauma, it's common to feel disconnected from your body, like it belongs to the past instead of the present. What's bringing this up for you now?"

I hesitated, the familiar knot of shame tightening in my stomach. "I guess… I've been experimenting. Trying to reclaim it." My fingers traced the hem of my sleeve. "I've been seeking out new ways to feel pleasure. Not for anyone else—just for me."

I glanced up, half-expecting judgment, but Dr. Monroe's face remained soft, encouraging.

"That's a really powerful step, Chelsea," she said. "Reconnecting with your body on *your* terms? That's healing."

I let out a shaky breath, relieved. "At first, I felt guilty. Like I wasn't supposed to enjoy this. Like my body wasn't *allowed* to feel good after everything." I swallowed hard. "But then I started thinking… Why should my trauma get to decide what I do with my body? Why should it have that power over me forever?"

Dr. Monroe's eyes softened. "It shouldn't," she said. "And it doesn't. Your body is *yours*, and you have every right to experience it in a way that feels safe, that feels good, that feels like *you* again."

I nodded, pressing my lips together. "I didn't think of it that way before. I thought healing had to look a certain way, like I had to earn my way back to feeling whole. But I think I'm realizing that healing is about *choice*. And I'm choosing this."

A small smile formed on her lips. "That's a huge shift, from guilt to permission. From survival to self-trust." She tilted her head slightly. "How does it feel, making that choice for yourself?"

I considered that for a moment. "Lighter," I admitted. "Like I don't have to carry the weight of what happened in the same way. Like I'm writing a new story for my body, instead of letting it be just a reminder of what was taken from me."

Dr. Monroe's voice was steady but full of warmth. "And you *are* writing a new story," she said. "One where you get to define what your body means to *you*."

I let that truth settle in my chest. My body was not just a battlefield, not just a collection of memories I had no say in. It was *mine*; and that meant I had the power to make it feel like home again.

With Daniel there was no pressure, no rushed expectations. As he would ask, "Why rush when you can indulge, lil' kitten? After all, a game of cat and mouse can be thrilling." Just long conversations where he asked questions no one had ever asked me before. About control. About limits. About trust.

I officially met him on a Tuesday.

Not that the day mattered, but I remember it because I had spent the whole morning debating whether or not to go through with it. My hands shook as I reapplied my lipstick for the third time, my nerves battling my curiosity.

Was I really doing this? Was I really about to have coffee with a man who called himself a *Dominant*?

It was just coffee. If I didn't like him, I could walk away. If I felt uncomfortable, I could ghost him like I had so many others. But somewhere inside my soul, I knew that wasn't true. Because this wasn't just a date; it was an unraveling. A step toward something I wasn't sure I was ready for, but couldn't resist any longer. This was how I was going to uncross the wires.

When I finally got out of the car, I spotted him immediately. He didn't look like Tray. That was the first thing I noticed. His presence wasn't loud or overwhelming. He didn't smirk at me like I was prey or stare at me with that possessive, all-knowing look that had once made my skin crawl. Instead, he watched me with a quiet intensity, his gaze steady, assessing. Not judging—*seeing*.

I walked up to him, feeling small and exposed, but also… alive.

"You're nervous," he said, his voice smooth, like he had all the time in the world.

I let out a breathless laugh. "A little."

He smiled, slow and knowing. "Good. That means you're taking this seriously."

I swallowed hard. I *was* taking this seriously. More seriously than I had taken anything in a long time. Because this wasn't just about meeting a man. This was about finding myself in the space between surrender and control.

And so the dance began and to describe such beauty I must use a metaphor…

* * *

A picture is painted upon the crisp breeze. With the wind ripping and flowing around me, I start to see it clearly. As if set in a scene of some distant memory, I just can't quite place it in time. Layers upon layers built upon themselves.

I start to see the trees despite the forest and each one is absolutely breathtaking. Drawn. Intrigued. Pulled away from my current space in time, I take a step deeper into this place of beauty. The powerful commandment of the space stops me in my tracks. Respect is now a given. I have a sense that it was earned long ago, and it deserves the recognition.

Shoes removed, I need the connection, to be grounded in this place, to truly understand it.

Step forward.

The perspicacity is magnificent. Penetration into my soul's mind is now something unavoidable. I know, I choose the step forward but the depth of observance is foreign. I find my mind cheering, almost celebrating the past's monotonous searching coming to an end. MORE is here.

Deep breath. Relaxed. Let us see what you can do. Elevated into the air and suspended above the treetops the stripping begins. Each part of myself I thought hidden carefully is grasped, taken, placed aside to be analyzed in greater detail. Detail it has always deserved but never experienced. Now suspended naked and exposed I only find myself feeling like an empty vessel, a beautiful treasure. Lowered back down in this state for now,

I step forward.

What a prodigious space. Moving pieces, chaos but yet in a perfectly coordinated way. I realize. This. This is a Dominant's mind. True to this fact, the strokes of the brush begin. Vibrant shades of all colors start to form a beautiful scene. I believe I see it clearly but as more strokes are made the picture unfolding before us starts to morph and change into something unforeseeable in wildest dreams.

The first piece of myself is presented. What an ugly thing, I instinctively shun away, avoiding eye contact with the mirror deposited before me. Chin now down, it is grasped and tilted upward, Kitten. My eyes shimmer from the glimpsing I attempt to conceal. Desperate, a word I have run from for what feels like a lifetime is whispered. It clings to the air, thick. Desperate. Do you feel the depths of this word? Not a grim unacceptable sentiment, I struggle to comprehend the new concept. How and where is the beauty?

Reluctance, deeper. Resistance, deeper. Tenacity, deeper. Perseverance. Lighting flashes with a loud thunderous sound to follow. Bewilderment behind my eyes I see the new crack form in the already shattered piece before me, an illusion?

The beauty is that this is an innate part of my soul. My soul and all it composes is what is shattered, not my heart; and this is what so desperately needs care, needs tending to, needs healing. Somehow this seemingly small piece is closer to fitting back into place then when it was originally removed, and I am in awe. Healed? Will you assist me in my path to completion?

I take a step forward.

One by one shattered pieces are presented. Discovery of not only this new mysterious forest around me but also the massive ocean within myself is all consuming. Waves and wind collide, crashing into each other. The trees are holding strong and steady despite the chaos. I find myself curious, breathing in and taking a glimpse around: What do I really see?

More.

I discovered I am not alone in this endeavor. It is time. I first grace my fingertips across the bark of the tree. The rough exterior has texture, has layers, just as the forest around me has depth. Then a subtle step into the waters, what did you see? Will the unimportant distractions fall like fog over this moment? Will it become so thick it is clouding our sight? NO. The waves come on the cusp of pleasure.

The forest comes to life, leaves are rustling, birds

singing, wild instinct evident. Nature is nature, and the two are synced.

We take a step deeper.

Riding the breeze soaring through the motions like a bird's feather. No longer attached to reality. No longer attached to the bird, the feather floats and whips and rides through this magical place. Seemingly free to take in every inch of its surroundings.

Let us look past the tough bark of the trees, let us see each vibrant color on the butterflies, let us take a rest in the grass to feel. Just to feel. All something out of a dream. That is the thing with dreams, we know it's inevitable we will wake. Yet here we are soaring, and why take away such a beautiful, free moment?

* * *

I NEVER THOUGHT I'D FEEL AT HOME IN MY OWN SKIN AGAIN. My body was a battleground, I carried my past like armor, heavy and suffocating, until I met him. Not a savior, not a knight—just a man who saw through the wreckage and understood that healing wasn't about stitching wounds, but letting them breathe.

With him, I danced a rhythm of trust and surrender, of push and pull, of reclaiming what was once stolen. Beneath the soft glow of flickering candlelight, I began to shed layers I thought were forever fused to my being. Each deliberate touch, each whispered command, became a roadmap back to myself. A gentle push here, a firm hand there. His mastery wasn't about control but about guiding me to reclaim my own.

It started subtly, the changes I felt outside the bedroom sessions. A glance in the mirror that lingered a little longer. Shoulders that once caved in now squared, daring the world to meet my gaze. I walked taller, my stride confident, hips swaying not in seduction but in certainty. Food was no longer just fuel to survive, but a celebration of this body I'd learned to adore. I rested, not out of exhaustion, but out of a newfound reverence for the vessel that carries my spirit.

A study published in *Sexual and Relationship Therapy* (2021) by Cory J. Cascalheira and colleagues found that BDSM can be a powerful tool for healing, especially for survivors of sexual trauma. Studies suggest that consensual BDSM engages neurological and psychological mechanisms that promote self-regulation, body awareness, and empowerment. The structured nature of BDSM— where boundaries are explicitly discussed and respected— can provide a sense of agency that many trauma survivors feel they have lost. Within this space, I was not at the mercy of past experiences; I was in control, negotiating my desires and limits with unwavering clarity.

Neurologically, these practices can trigger altered states of consciousness similar to those experienced in mindfulness and meditation. The rhythmic, intentional nature of impact play, restraint, or sensory deprivation can induce a "flow state," lowering cortisol levels and increasing endorphins, much like deep meditation or intense exercise. Some researchers have even likened subspace—the euphoric, trance-like state some submissives experience—to the dissociative states that trauma survivors are familiar with, but with one crucial difference: This time, I chose to enter it. I *trusted* the experience, the person guiding me through it, and most importantly, myself.

Beyond the physiological shifts, they can also be deeply reparative on an emotional level. Engaging in trust-based dynamics allowed me to rewrite my relationship with power. Where once power had been taken from me, now it was something I willingly handed over in carefully negotiated terms, knowing I had the right to withdraw it at any moment. The process was not about recreating trauma, but about reclaiming my body, my boundaries, and my pleasure—proving to myself that I was not broken, that my body was not a crime scene, but a place where I could still experience joy and safety.

I had spent years feeling like my body was something that had been *done to*. But now, standing in front of the mirror, I saw something different. My body was *mine* again. Not just in whispers, not just in fleeting moments, but in every confident step I took into the world.

It taught me that surrender was not defeat but liberation. In the ebb and flow of our dance, I discovered the symphony of my desires—loud, unapologetic, and mine to conduct.

I thought I needed saving. Instead, I found a man willing to stand beside me while I saved myself, one command, one touch, one heartbeat at a time.

Our time was never meant to last forever. That was the unspoken truth woven between every touch, every whispered command, every moment he held me steady while I learned to stand on my own. He never claimed me; not in the way others had, not in the way I once feared. He simply reminded me, again and again, that I had always belonged to myself.

The night we said goodbye, there were no grand gestures, no desperate pleas to hold onto something that had already served its purpose. Instead, he took my hand, and with complete soft, gentle confidence he gave me my key. The key I had once surrendered to him in trembling hands, believing I was offering him control. "It was always yours," he said, his voice steady, reverent. "You just weren't ready to see it."

And I understood. I had come to him lost, drowning in the echoes of my past, believing I needed someone to save me. But what he had given me was not salvation, it was a mirror, reflecting the power I had buried beneath my fear. He never kept me in chains; he taught me how to wear them like jewelry, how to let them become symbols of my strength rather than reminders of my captivity.

So, when he walked away, I didn't break. I didn't collapse into the emptiness I once feared would swallow me whole. Instead, I stood taller. I breathed deeper. I lived louder.

The time was over, but the gift remained. My freedom. My voice. My body, no longer a battleground but a sanctuary.

Chapter Eight

CALLOUSED HANDS

I had to heal this time, Love. My mind, body, and soul was left damaged seemingly beyond repair. However, even when the entire forest burns down, new life will appear in time.

I worked hard at repairing myself; I had wasted enough time already.

What I didn't know, Love, is you were there the whole time helping me.

You came upon me like sunlight through my children. I was planting in rich soil given to me from my mother, watered by friends, dreams, and experience. I pulled away all the dead parts, letting go of my pain. I grew new life within and around me till I was a rich forest more beautiful than ever before.

Looking around, Love, I finally felt complete, but you were not done.

You came upon me once more like a breeze. Gently you flowed through my forest, around my trees, caressing my flowers. You didn't have any interest in being destructive or in changing but rather in admiration of what I had grown. Strong and stubborn, I stood my ground making note of your presence but not recognition. It wasn't until the fall that I realized it was you, Love.

I had continued to grow and was now in the process of shedding my leaves. Few holding on for dear life, not realizing that their presence would prevent new growth. This is when the breeze came along helping them to the ground.

As seasons changed you were still present, Love. Gliding through my forest, you touched every part of me once again. Yet, this time you did not cause destruction. I knew you could, wind can be very powerful, but you didn't.

On the days your breeze was not there and the forest was still, there was beauty and life, but not as lovely. You enhanced my world, Love, and I wanted you there. I found myself longing for your caressing kiss to my cheeks, your playful nature, your calming presence; a love I didn't know existed. I found myself naturally looking for you each day.

Now in harmony we have each other everyday. You, My Love, are defined in your calming presence, defined in my knowing you are there, but so am I. We dance with each other by choice. Everyday I find myself sitting at the edge of the forest, standing on a mountain waiting to feel your kiss upon my cheek. Ready to face the new day together.

For eleven years, Andreas had been my tattoo artist, my silent witness. He had inked my skin while my ex hovered close, ensuring our conversations never went beyond the necessary. I never let myself *see* him beyond his work, beyond the safety of the transactional. He was my artist, nothing more.

But as I stepped into the tattoo shop, the familiar hum of machines in the air, I knew this was different. This wasn't just another appointment. This was a mark of survival. The poppy, a symbol of rebirth after death, would be my *soul center tattoo,* blooming over the skin I had reclaimed as my own.

For years, I had been trapped in Wonderland, where nothing was what it seemed; where love twisted itself into something suffocating. Every move was watched, every connection controlled. Even here, in this shop, I had always felt like I existed behind an invisible barrier— because Andreas was a man and that had been enough to make him a threat.

But now?

Now, I was free. And for the first time, I saw him, not just as the man holding the needle, but as a man.

And that was a problem.

He had changed over the years, or maybe I was only seeing him fully for the first time. Over six feet, lean but strong. His dreads spilled over his shoulders, dark ropes falling around his face that looked both dangerous and inviting, his skin a warm mix of hues that made me wonder about the places and people who had shaped him. Those eyes—framed by dermal piercings that caught the light—held something sharp, something knowing. He looked like a wolf, all edge and power. But I had a feeling there was something softer beneath the surface.

And this time, there was no one standing between us.

My heart—a hard, cold shell after everything I had been through—tightened like a fist. I was done with bad boys, done with smooth voices and sharp smirks, done with the risk of letting anyone close.

This was business.

I set my chin and stepped forward, refusing to let my gaze linger. He was just my artist, the same as he had always been. Nothing more.

He looked up as I approached, and our eyes met without barriers. Without permission needing to be granted.

His head tilted slightly, and a slow smirk tugged at the corner of his lips.

"You probably don't recognize me," I said, my voice smooth, confidence wrapped around each word like silk. I moved with the sway of a vixen, the kind of woman I had rebuilt myself to be—untouchable, unreadable.

His gaze didn't waver, didn't flicker with confusion or hesitation.

"I know exactly who you are." His voice was steady,

certain. Like a man who never questioned what he saw. "I remember your eyes."

My heart clenched.

He had seen me before. But not like this. Not on the other side. Standing there, exposed yet unafraid, I felt like Dorothy stepping out of her black-and-white world into Oz, where everything pulsed with color, alive with possibility. I was no longer the timid girl clutching at fragments of myself. I was vibrant, undeniable, unhidden. The shift was almost cinematic, as if the air itself shimmered differently around me. His eyes told me he noticed it too; that this wasn't the same version of me he had once known, but someone reborn, radiant in her own power.

One consultation and two appointments later, and he was inviting me to coffee.

Not just with him, though. No, this wasn't about trying to get in my pants.

He leaned against the counter, arms crossed over his chest, watching me with that same steady, unreadable gaze. "A group of us meet for coffee every morning," he said casually, like it was nothing. Like it wasn't something that felt entirely too personal coming from him. "Didn't you say you were looking to make friends? If you ever want to pass through, I'll be there."

I hesitated, searching his face for some kind of ulterior motive, some hint that this was a line, a setup for something more. But there was nothing, just an open invitation.

The old me, fresh from the wreckage of Wonderland and still wary of every hidden turn, wanted to decline, to keep my walls firmly in place.

But the new me? The one still learning what it meant to stand in Oz, to trust my own instincts again?

She was curious.

That morning, I almost didn't go. Coffee was mine— my ritual, my solitude. But something in me wanted to test what might bloom if I let myself step into someone else's rhythm.

On the way, I spotted a dandelion growing stubbornly between cracks in the sidewalk. I plucked it, held it a moment, then blew. Off upon the breeze went each of the little white seeds, scattering to places unseen, carrying wishes into the air. Wishes for me, maybe, or perhaps planting flowers for someone else to stumble upon, creating wishing opportunities for another.

I laughed, shaking my head. So childish, I thought. Yet, so thrilling.

As I gathered my bag, I tried to gather my thoughts too. They were scattered, unmoored. Normally, I'd have prepared a dozen conversation scripts in my mind, rehearsed replies to imagined questions. But I had nothing. Absolutely nothing.

Fuck it. We'll be as spontaneous as this entire encounter is.

I need coffee.

The shop was quieter than I expected, the kind of quiet

that hums with its own presence. Click, click, click—
my heels tapped against the worn wood floor. Perhaps I
shouldn't have worn heels. Too tall, I worried. No, I told
myself, not too tall. Just me.

My mind wandered as I went through the mundane
steps—breathing, walking, adjusting the strap on my
shoulder.

And then the door creaked open, and I saw them.
The group, my purpose for this small leap into the un-
familiar.

Cheeks flush. *Shit.*

I'd like to imagine I floated gracefully to my seat, but
in truth it felt more like a stutter. A rock skipping across
a serene lake, rippling the calm. No one seemed to mind
my disruption.

Conversation began to flow, not forced but natural.
Like a violin—beautiful, simple, yet with an odd, imperfect
rhythm. There were skips and screeches, laughter that
tripped over itself, pauses that somehow worked.

I started to glimpse their minds, their souls even.
Some guarded behind locked doors. Some with doorways
deliberately stripped of hinges, wide open for anyone to
walk through. Long tunnels, vast open rooms, pieces of
humanity laid bare over mugs of steaming coffee.

I kept feeling like something was just out of reach,
floating on the breeze. I tried to keep up, but eventually
forgot I was even chasing, caught instead by the unfolding
moment.

My body responded in ways long forgotten, heart racing, breath uneven, brain sparking like Christmas lights. Time ticked by not fast, not slow, but as if it belonged to another universe altogether.

Another wave hit me, was I chasing something? Or was I simply floating? It didn't feel stressful or daunting. It felt peaceful. Like a dandelion seed drifting on a spring breeze. And I couldn't help but wonder where it would land.

It was during these mornings that I unknowingly began walking the lessons of the Tin Man, the Lion, and the Scarecrow.

It started with an old friend. Sam.

I hadn't seen her in years, not since the slow unraveling of our friendship. She had also been there through Tray… had seen the ugliness, had warned me, had tried to pull me away before I was ready to see the truth myself. In the end, he had been the wedge that split us apart.

Yet, when I ran into her one morning, it was like stepping through a doorway into a version of myself I had almost forgotten. There was no hesitation in her smile, no resentment in the way she hugged me. And just like that, we picked up where we left off, except now, I was different. Stronger.

Andreas, Sam, and I started moving through summer like a pack of strays who had found their way back home. Mornings became a ritual—walking Forsyth Park, our footsteps slow and steady against the pavement, the

Spanish moss overhead swaying like it knew secrets we were just beginning to learn.

Through them, I faced the lessons I hadn't yet realized I needed.

The Tin Man's heart: I had locked mine away for so long, convinced it was better to feel nothing than to risk pain. But walking beside Andreas, hearing his laugh, watching the way his eyes softened when he listened—really listened—challenged that numbness.

The Lion's courage: Sam had always been bold, never afraid to say what was on her mind. She reminded me what it meant to stand firm, to take up space, to not apologize for existing.

The Scarecrow's wisdom: It came in pieces, in quiet revelations as I sat across from Andreas in the early morning light, realizing that intelligence wasn't just knowing facts. It was knowing yourself. And I was still learning.

I told myself it was just coffee. Just friendship. Just morning walks in the summer heat.

But something was shifting. And I wasn't sure I was ready for it.

As summer faded, so did the ease of it all.

Sam moved away in early autumn, chasing a new adventure. We promised to keep in touch, but we both knew how life had a way of unraveling even the best intentions. Our trio became a duo, and as the mornings turned colder, the group that had once filled coffee shops and park paths dwindled until it was just me and Andreas.

It was a coincidence. Just timing.

We kept meeting, kept walking Forsyth even as the air turned crisp and the trees shed their leaves in slow surrender. The laughter came easier, the silences more comfortable. I learned the way his legs crossed when he spoke, how his voice could turn rich and low when he was lost in thought. I noticed the way his eyes crinkled just slightly at the edges when he smiled, a real smile, not the cocky smirk he often wore like armor.

And slowly, his life started to open up to me.

I knew, without him ever having to say it, that there was someone else. Or, rather, there *had been.* A relationship that had long since hollowed out but hadn't quite ended. The way he spoke about her, when he did, was careful, too careful. The kind of careful that comes from years of walking on eggshells.

"She's moving out soon," he told me one morning, his breath visible in the cold air as we walked the park loop. His voice was casual, but his eyes gave him away—tired, relieved, and something else I couldn't quite name.

"That's… good, right?" I asked, though I wasn't sure if I was asking for him or for myself.

"Yeah," he said after a pause, exhaling like he was finally putting down a weight he'd carried too long. "It's been over for a while. Just… took some time to make it official."

I understood that more than I wanted to. How a relationship could die long before the people in it found the courage to bury it.

But understanding didn't make it easier.

Because as he untangled himself from her, I felt the invisible line between us growing thinner. And I hated it.

I hated how easy it was to be near him. How safe it felt.

Safe was an illusion. *Safe* was a lie I had told myself before, right before the world cracked open beneath my feet.

So, I fought it.

I fought it with cold, calculated logic, running through a list of reasons why this—*we*—could never be more than what it was. He was too much of a "bad boy," too different from the life I told myself I should have. The life I had meticulously planned, as if love could be mapped out in neat, predictable lines. I convinced myself that attraction was just that; something fleeting, something I could ignore, something that would pass like the seasons.

But love doesn't work like that.

It seeped in through the cracks I refused to acknowledge. It settled in the spaces between our conversations, in the way he paid attention, in the way he never pushed but was always *there*.

And little by little, despite every wall I put up, despite every reason I gave myself to turn away—I started to feel more.

It ended quietly, the final thread of a worn-out relationship unraveling in the way it was always meant to.

One day, she was still in his space, lingering like a ghost in a house she no longer belonged to. And then, she wasn't.

He didn't celebrate it, didn't rush to fill the empty space with something—or someone—new. He simply *breathed*. And I noticed it, the way his shoulders sat lighter, the way his laughter came easier.

And still, I told myself this wasn't anything more than friendship.

But chemistry has a way of ignoring reason.

*   *   *

Purple, crisp yet unclear simultaneously.

Images that take on a life of their own. As if they grew legs and started doing a jig.

The opposite of all that is rational.

What is rational?

I make my way through this scene and stroll at a pace to only observe.

Large trees. My eyes follow from the base to the tops of the branches. They reach for the sun. They have shades of green I have never noticed. The sunlight peeking through as if saying hello.

I continue,

Now I notice Joy walking alongside me. This sensation hasn't been around in a while, now grown a persona of its own and joining me?

A secret garden appears. How can you be so public, yet private. Going unnoticed by the masses. Roses bloom, water trickles. It feels safe here inside these walls.

Allowing the force field that are my walls to take a rest.

I continue,

Now Creativity walks alongside me.

I take note of ruins in the distance. A glass castle that once shined with colors so beautiful now seems dangerous and painful. Some parts are completely shattered. Jagged edges, warning anyone who has an inkling to come close that pain is sure to follow.

I break my focus on these ruins when I see Creativity start to skip along the path.

Before us appears a field of dandelions and daisies.

Eyes wide, my first instinct is to make a wish.

Ignoring any doubt I pick one and blow.

I'm suddenly innocent. Taking on the carefree spirit of a child; I sit cross legged in the grass and watch. The seeds float upon the breeze and I feel peace, I feel hope. Eloquently the seeds become koi fish swimming through the air, beautiful colors of orange glisten in the sunlight. A little orange heart floats down and lands in my grasp.

I continue,

Now Peace walks alongside.

I come across a large fountain. It's loud but the bustling around it is seemingly louder.

Suddenly the image of the glass castle ruins appears. I become panicked, scared.

Everything is so loud now.

I walk to a nearby bench. I sit there staring Joy, Creativity, and Peace in the eyes.

Then I hear it. The water from the fountain. I close my eyes and focus on nothing else. Everything around us disappears, and I am reminded that when things are chaotic I simply need to focus.

I stand and continue,

Now You are beside me. We are talking of everything and nothing as Joy, Creativity, and Peace feel safe enough to simply be.

* * *

IT WAS IN THE WAY OUR CONVERSATIONS STRETCHED LONGER, in the way he remembered the little things I mentioned in passing. Like buying me an umbrella because he noticed I didn't have one but often was dressed nicely for work. It was in the way he looked at me, not with the hunger of a man chasing conquest, but with the quiet knowing of someone who *saw* me.

But the moment that cracked something deep in me? It wasn't about us at all. It was about my kids.

He met them not as some man I was dating, not as someone I was trying to fit into our world but as a friend. Someone safe.

And when I watched him with them, something inside me softened.

He was patient. He listened. He laughed with them like they were the best company in the world. And I realized, *they deserved this.* They deserved a love that wasn't complicated by pain. They deserved the kind of presence that wasn't fleeting or conditional.

And maybe, *so did I.*

But even then, I held back.

Because falling for a man like him, a man who led with kindness, who didn't *need* to prove his strength with force, felt too easy. Too dangerous in its own way.

But he never rushed me. Never pressed.

Instead, he showed me.

Every time he held a door open, every time he carried the baby's car seat without me asking, every time he reached for something so I didn't have to, he showed me.

And my once-calloused hands, rough from years of doing it all on my own, from *having* to, they started to soften.

And so did my heart.

* * *

FALLING IN LOVE DIDN'T HAPPEN ALL AT ONCE. IT WASN'T A lightning strike, sudden and shocking. It was slow, like the tide creeping in, washing over me inch by inch until I looked around and realized I was surrounded by it.

Moving with him to Savannah felt like stepping into a life I hadn't dared imagine for myself. Stability. Safety. Love that wasn't something I had to chase or *prove* I was worthy of. It was just *there.* It was in the way Lillie found her place, making new friends, her world stretching open in ways I had feared it never would. We hired a tutor, and suddenly, school wasn't something she dreaded. She *thrived.* It was the way he encouraged Abbie to take her first steps. It wasn't just mornings together and long conversations that bled into the night.

It was *home.*

But love didn't erase fear.

One night, long after the girls had gone to bed, it crept in. That old whisper, the one that told me I wasn't meant for this. That I had spent so long fighting to be free, how could I now let myself be *kept?*

I wasn't done having my adventure.

And the thought of a relationship—of permanence— felt like a door closing.

I broke down. Sat on the floor of our bedroom, knees pulled to my chest, panic clawing up my throat.

"I don't know if I can do this," I admitted. "What if I lose myself? What if I wake up one day and realize I don't belong here?"

He didn't try to convince me, didn't tell me I was being ridiculous or selfish.

Instead, he asked, "Then what do you need?"

And that was how, instead of leaving, instead of running from the thing that scared me most, I found myself boarding a plane to Greece.

Alone.

Andreas helped make it happen. He held down the

fort, took care of the kids, and made sure everything kept running smoothly.

He *wanted* me to go. Not because he wanted space, but because he knew *I* needed it.

Because he loved me enough to give me the freedom I was so afraid of losing.

Chapter Nine

SILENCE

My most reflective moments usually happened when I was alone. For years, solitude had been a stranger to me—my only real moments with it were stolen inside the steam of long showers, where the water carried away my tears like a secret. Every other part of my life was filled with sound: children calling, dishes clattering, phones buzzing, men's voices pulling pieces of me I didn't want to give. I was terrified of silence because it meant sitting with my own thoughts, and my own thoughts used to feel like a prison.

But in Athens, somewhere between the chatter of my mind and the stillness of true aloneness, I stumbled onto something else. Change. Not sudden or loud, but steady, like sunlight inching across a room.

It was beautiful and devastating all at once.

I mourned the innocence of the girl I had been before the darkness. The girl who believed in love with open hands, who saw the world through unclouded glass. She was gone, shattered by what she endured. Yet she lived inside me still, a ghost in my marrow. I carried her grief and her hope together, a paradox that made me both fragile and unshakable.

I thought of the first time I ever ate in a restaurant alone, after my divorce, when solitude felt like an accusation. I ordered food, sat upright, tried not to notice my own nervous hands. But then, between sips of my drink, I found myself watching strangers: couples leaning close, an old man reading a paper, a child with sticky fingers giggling at the world. And I wondered what they carried beneath their ordinary moments. Were they, too, hiding secret heartbreaks stitched under their skin? That night I learned something, aloneness wasn't emptiness. It was curiosity. It was a doorway.

Years later, waiting in an airport with a ticket to Greece in my hand, I promised myself that by the end of the trip I would be fluent in the art of being alone.

And so I wandered.

Through narrow alleyways where laundry lines crisscrossed overhead like ribbons in the sky. Through streets that twisted like veins, the smell of fresh bread drifting from bakeries, the hum of mopeds weaving through crowds. Each turn was an act of surrender. Even dead ends offered gifts: a potted basil plant warming in the sun, a grandmother shaking linen into the wind, a stray cat stretched out like royalty on cool stone steps.

One morning, I climbed the hill to a centuries-old monastery. The air grew thinner as I ascended, the sound of the city falling away until only cicadas hummed in the trees. The monastery walls were worn with age, their stones the color of ash and honey. Inside, the air was cool, heavy with the scent of beeswax and incense. Candles flickered in quiet rows, each flame a whisper of someone's prayer. I lit one too, not begging for escape, as I once would have, but asking for presence. For courage to stand where I was, scars and all, without apology. The silence there did not suffocate me. It soothed. It was the kind of silence that holds you like a mother rocking a child.

Another day, I boarded the ferry to Poros. The sea stretched wide as glass, the salt mist clinging to my skin as if to mark me alive. The ferry creaked and swayed, gulls circling above, their cries sharp against the endless horizon. On the island, I found a flat rock that jutted out of the water, and I climbed out onto it. The waves lapped at its edges, cool and rhythmic, like the earth's own heartbeat. I pulled out my paints and began to create and not for anyone else, not for validation, but because color felt like breath in my chest. I painted with the sea at my feet, the sun at my back; I wasn't painting over pain. I was painting possibility. That rock became my cathedral. The sea, my congregation. The brush, my prayer.

That trip wasn't only about places, it was about people.

One evening, I met Marta, a friend of Maja's, for dinner in the city. I had only heard stories of her before, yet when she walked in, I felt as if I had always known her. She had the kind of presence that filled a room without trying:

sparkling eyes, bracelets chiming softly as she gestured, a laugh that cracked open the air.

We sat at a little café tucked into a vine-covered corner, plates of roasted lamb and fresh olives between us. Conversation poured easily, like wine into waiting glasses. She told me about her years working in the Middle East during war, about holding her ground in the auto industry when women were barely welcomed at the table. Her stories carried grit and freedom, the kind that can only come from living fully and refusing to shrink.

At one point, she leaned forward, swirling the wine in her glass. "I'd rather feel lonely alone than lonely in a relationship," she said, her voice steady but kind. "Because that kind of lonely—when you're sitting beside someone who doesn't really see you—that's far worse."

Her words pierced me, because I knew that loneliness intimately. The kind where you can't breathe even as someone sleeps beside you.

I nodded slowly. "I think that's what I'm learning. How to sit with myself and not feel empty. To enjoy my own company."

Her lips curved into a smile. "Exactly. You find yourself first, and then the right people can only add to that. They don't complete you, they meet you where you're already whole."

She raised her glass, her bracelets catching the candlelight. "Life is complicated, darling. But being true to yourself—that's the simplest, hardest thing you'll ever do."

Our glasses clinked, and for the rest of the evening we talked as if we had carried the same storms in different seas. By the time we left, I realized Marta hadn't just told me her story, she had given me a mirror. A glimpse of the woman I was becoming.

Later that week, in the cool halls of the National Archaeological Museum, I found myself in front of a marble goddess, her form chipped and fractured, yet her stance unyielding. When the guide told me she was a goddess of protection, revered for centuries not despite her brokenness but because of her endurance, something opened in me. Broken, yes. But powerful because of it. I touched my chest and whispered, "Me too."

Strangers mirrored that lesson back to me too. Two young women at a café with crisp accents and easy laughter folded me into their circle like I belonged. When one of them called me "inspiring," I nearly choked on the word. I had been called strong, yes. A survivor, yes. But inspiring? That word settled in me like a seed.

And one night, as music swelled through the theater during *Phantom of the Opera*, I felt it—that shift. The music filled me, lifted me, and I realized I was not afraid anymore. I was whole in my own company.

When Andreas called me after the show, asking if I was happy, I thought of the goddess statue, of the monastery candle, of the rock in the sea where I painted, of Marta's words about loneliness, of the girl I once was who trembled at the thought of being alone.

"Yes," I whispered, my voice catching with truth. "I really am."

By the time I returned to Savannah, I was not unrecognizable. I was still me—the mother, the friend, the woman—but I was more. More alive. More grounded. More whole than I had ever dared to believe possible.

I had walked through violence, through silence, through the wreckage of who I thought I was. I had carried years of fear like stones in my pockets, yet somehow, I learned to set them down. My scars were no longer chains. They were inscriptions of survival, like cracks in marble that proved time, endurance, and power.

This was my full circle.

Not an ending, but a threshold.

A life no longer defined by survival, but by freedom. No longer running from silence, but resting in it. No longer fractured, but whole—precisely because of the fractures.

Healing, I learned, is not linear. It is messy, it is tender, it is two steps forward and one back.

It is sitting across from a therapist who hands you tools when all you feel you hold are broken pieces.

It is relearning how to breathe when your body has spent years bracing for impact.

It is discovering that your worth was never tied to who loved you or who hurt you, but to the unshakable truth that you are still here.

If I could reach back and hold the hand of the woman I once was—the one who second-guessed every word, who shrank to keep the peace, who believed loneliness beside someone was better than loneliness alone—I would tell her this:

You are allowed to take up space.

You are allowed to start over.

You are allowed to demand joy, not just survival.

And I remembered Marta's words, still echoing in me like a hymn: *Better lonely alone than lonely beside someone who cannot see you.*

Like the goddess, like the monastery walls, like the sea itself, I remain. Weathered, enduring, alive.

And that, I have learned, is its own kind of divinity.

* * *

I STEPPED OUT OF THE CONFERENCE HALL AND INTO THE humid Savannah evening, the heat clinging to my skin like a second layer. My heels clicked against the pavement as I made my way to my car, my mind racing, thoughts overlapping in a tangled web of emotions. I pulled out my phone and dialed Andreas.

The line rang twice before his familiar voice answered. "Hey, Chelsea. Everything okay?"

I let out a breath I hadn't realized I was holding. "Yeah. Yeah, I just—I needed to talk to someone. Can you meet me?"

"Of course," he said without hesitation. "Where?"

"That little café on Broughton. The one with the patio."

"I'll be there in fifteen."

Fifteen minutes later, I was seated at an outside table, absentmindedly stirring the melting ice in my water glass. The streetlights above cast a warm glow, and the distant hum of cars and conversations blended into white noise.

When Andreas arrived, he took one look at me and knew something was up. "Alright, spill."

I exhaled sharply. "The conference was... different than I expected." I paused, gathering my thoughts. "I went in feeling like I belonged there, like I was one of them. Confident. In control. And then—then this speaker started talking about the benefits cliff. And suddenly, I wasn't just a professional in a fitted black dress, shaking hands with CEOs and making connections. I was that girl again, sitting in a trailer with no stove, no finished floors, no certainty. I was the single mom staring at a paycheck, trying to decide whether a raise was worth losing childcare."

Andreas leaned forward, his brow furrowed. "That must have hit hard."

"It did. And not just because I've lived it—because I'd never framed it that way before. Never really thought of my past as a set of hurdles I had to clear just to be in that room today. I always thought it was just... life. But listening to her, it was like someone held up a mirror, and I saw every version of myself staring back. The little girl. The scared young wife. The mother clawing her way forward."

He was quiet for a moment, letting my words settle between us. "Sounds like it wasn't just a conference. Sounds like a reckoning."

I huffed a small laugh. "Yeah. Something like that. But it wasn't just about realizing how far I've come. It was about understanding why I fight so hard to keep moving forward. It's not just for me—it's for my kids. For other women who are standing at the edge of that cliff, trying to decide if jumping is worth the fall."

Andreas nodded, his expression thoughtful. "So, what now?"

I leaned back, stretching my legs beneath the table. "Now? Now I make sure my voice isn't just heard in those rooms—I make sure it matters. I don't just exist in these spaces; I shape them. I advocate, I mentor, I lift others up. Because if I can pull myself over that cliff, I sure as hell can build a bridge for the next woman."

A slow smile spread across Andreas' face. "That's the Chelsea I know."

I smirked, taking a sip of my water. "Damn right it is."

About the Author

Chelsea Simpson is an author, speaker, and communications professional based in Savannah, Georgia, where she is raising her two daughters and building a life rooted in reflection, growth, and intentional forward movement. She brings honesty, depth, and lived experience to conversations about resilience, healing, and the power of shared stories.

A survivor of domestic abuse, Chelsea knows firsthand the strength required to break cycles and choose something different. Her writing explores family patterns, vulnerability, and the quiet courage it takes to speak what was once held in silence. She believes healing happens in community—when we tell the truth, listen deeply, and allow ourselves to be seen.

When she is not writing or speaking, Chelsea finds grounding in time with her children, the outdoors, and moments that slow life down. Those moments continue to shape the perspective and care she brings to her work.

www.ingramcontent.com/pod-product-compliance
Lightning Source LLC
Chambersburg PA
CBHW070932130626
46555CB00001B/404